The Smartest Words Ever Spoken

1001 Timeless Quotes

Compiled by Lee Jenkins

ABC
PUBLISHING
A BETTER CHOICE PUBLISHING

The Smartest Words Ever Spoken:
1001 Timeless Quotes

A Better Choice Publishing
41 Temperance Street, P.O. Box 2
Clarington, ON L1C 3A0   Canada
Sales Information: sales@abcpublishing.org

Library and Archives Canada Cataloguing in Publication

The smartest words ever spoken : 1001 timeless quotes / compiled by Lee Jenkins.

Issued also in an electronic format.
ISBN 978-0-9866789-3-6

1. Quotations, English. 2. Motivation (Psychology)-- Quotations, maxims, etc. I. Jenkins, Lee, 1959—

PN6084.S45S62 2010   082   C2010-906736-3

To all my Facebook page fans.
You continue to inspire me with your comments and show that
a positive attitude is the start of all good things.
http://www.facebook.com/ConceiveBelieveAchieve

To Gretchen, who understands, inspires
and puts up with me.

I've always been inspired by the timeless thoughts of others who seem to have been able to shed the shackles of worldliness and bring their minds to a higher plane. They raise my mental state, help me aspire higher, think bigger and become the person I know I can be.

I know this collection of some of my favorites will do the same for you.

CONTENTS

ACCEPTANCE

1. "When you find peace within yourself, you become the kind of person who can live at peace with others."
   —*Peace Pilgrim*

2. "Many of us crucify ourselves between two thieves—regret for the past and fear of the future."
   —*Fulton Oursler*

3. "Being happy doesn't mean that everything is perfect. It means that you've decided to look beyond the imperfections."
   —*Unknown*

4. "As you become more clear about who you really are, you'll be better able to decide what is best for you—the first time around."
   —*Oprah Winfrey*

5. "Deep down even the most hardened criminal is starving for the same thing that motivates the innocent baby: Love and acceptance."
   —*Lily Fairchilde*

6. "A true man never frets about his place in the world, but just slides into it by the gravitation of his nature, and swings there as easily as a star."
   —*Edwin Hubbel Chapin*

7. "Some people confuse acceptance with apathy, but there's all the difference in the world. Apathy fails to distinguish between what can and what cannot be helped; acceptance makes that distinction. Apathy paralyzes the will-to-action; acceptance frees it by relieving it of impossible burdens."
   —*Arthur Gordon*

8. "The art of acceptance is the art of making someone who has just done you a small favor wish that he might have done you a greater one."
—*Martin Luther King, Jr.*

9. "That is the definition of faith—acceptance of that which we imagine to be true, that which we cannot prove."
—*Dan Brown*

10. "California sunlight—sweet Calcutta rain—Honolulu starbright—the song remains the same."
—*Led Zeppelin*

11. "But there isn't any second half of myself waiting to plug in and make me whole. It's there. I'm already whole."
—*Sally Field*

12. "Acceptance is not submission; it is acknowledgement of the facts of a situation. Then deciding what you're going to do about it."
—*Kathleen Casey Theisen*

13. "If a ship has been sunk, I can't bring it up. If it is going to be sunk, I can't stop it. I can use my time much better working on tomorrow's problem than by fretting about yesterday's. Besides, if I let those things get me, I wouldn't last long."
—*Admiral Ernest J. King*

14. "The only thing that will make you happy is being happy with who you are, and not who people think you are."
—*Goldie Hawn*

15. "Acceptance and tolerance and forgiveness, those are life-altering lessons."
—*Jessica Lange*

16. "Acceptance is not love. You love a person because he or she has lovable traits, but you accept everybody just because they're alive and human."
—*Albert Ellis*

17. "Acceptance of one's life has nothing to do with resignation; it does not mean running away from the struggle. On the contrary, it means accepting it as it comes, with all the handicaps of heredity, of suffering, of psychological complexes and injustices."
—*Paul Tournier*

18. "Acceptance of what has happened is the first step to overcoming the consequences of any misfortune."
—*William James*

19. "At the heart of personality is the need to feel a sense of being lovable without having to qualify for that acceptance."
—*Paul Tournier*

20. "Happiness can exist only in acceptance."
—*George Orwell*

21. "The first step toward change is awareness. The second step is acceptance."
—*Nathaniel Branden*

22. "The greatest gift that you can give to others is the gift of unconditional love and acceptance."
—*Brian Tracy*

23. "The keys to patience are acceptance and faith. Accept things as they are, and look realistically at the world around you. Have faith in yourself and in the direction you have chosen."
—*Ralph Marston*

ACHIEVEMENT

24. "When we think of failure; failure will be ours. If we remain undecided; nothing will ever change. All we need to do is want to achieve something great and then simply to do it. Never think of failure—for what we think, will come about."
    —*Maharishi Mahesh Yogi*

25. "The results you achieve will be in direct proportion to the effort you apply."
    —*Denis Waitley*

26. "The truth of the matter is that there's nothing you can't accomplish if: (1) You clearly decide what it is that you're absolutely committed to achieving, (2) You're willing to take massive action, (3) You notice what's working or not, and (4) You continue to change your approach until you achieve what you want, using whatever life gives you along the way."
    —*Anthony Robbins*

27. "That some achieve great success, is proof to all that others can achieve it as well."
    —*Abraham Lincoln*

28. "All great achievements require time."
    —*David J. Schwartz*

29. "My mother drew a distinction between achievement and success. She said that achievement is the knowledge that you have studied and worked hard and done the best that is in you. Success is being praised by others. That is nice but not as important or satisfying. Always aim for achievement and forget about success."
—*Helen Hayes*

30. "Where I was born and where and how I have lived is unimportant. It is what I have done with where I have been that should be of interest."
—*Georgia O'Keeffe*

31. "When your desires are strong enough, you will appear to possess superhuman powers to achieve."
—*Napoleon Hill*

32. "All that a man achieves and all that he fails to achieve is the direct result of his own thoughts."
—*James Allen*

33. "You never achieve success unless you like what you are doing."
—*Dale Carnegie*

34. "Those who dare to fail miserably can achieve greatly."
—*John Fitzgerald Kennedy*

35. "What we achieve inwardly will change outer reality."
—*Plutarch*

36. "No one lives long enough to learn everything they need to learn starting from scratch. To be successful, we absolutely, positively have to find people who have already paid the price to learn the things that we need to learn to achieve our goals."
—*Brian Tracy*

37. "You have all the reason in the world to achieve your grandest dreams. Imagination plus innovation equals realization."
—*Denis Waitley*

38. "With our eyes fixed on the future, but recognizing the realities of today, we will achieve our destiny to be as a shining city on a hill for all mankind to see."
—*Ronald Reagan*

39. "Think of yourself as on the threshold of unparalleled success. A whole, clear, glorious life lies before you. Achieve! Achieve!."
—*Andrew Carnegie*

40. "One must marry one's feelings to one's beliefs and ideas. That is probably the only way to achieve a measure of harmony in one's life."
—*Napoleon Hill*

41. "You cannot expect to achieve new goals or move beyond your present circumstances unless you change."
—*Les Brown*

42. "The person determined to achieve maximum success learns the principle that progress is made one step at a time. A house is built one brick at a time. Football games are won a play at a time. A department store grows bigger one customer at a time. Every big accomplishment is a series of little accomplishments."
—*David Joseph Schwartz*

43. "The three great essentials to achieve anything worthwhile are, first, hard work; second, stick-to-itiveness; third, common sense."
—*Thomas Alva Edison*

44. "Nothing average ever stood as a monument to progress. When progress is looking for a partner it doesn't turn to those who believe they are only average. It turns instead to those who are forever searching and striving to become the best they possibly can. If we seek the average level we cannot hope to achieve a high level of success. Our only hope is to avoid being a failure."
—*A. Lou Vickery*

45. "Be not afraid of greatness; some are born great, some achieve greatness, and others have greatness thrust upon them."
—*William Shakespeare*

46. "Determine what specific goal you want to achieve. Then dedicate yourself to its attainment with unswerving singleness of purpose, the trenchant zeal of a crusader."
—*Paul J. Meyer*

47. "You will achieve [your] grand dream, a day at a time, so set goals for each day—not long and difficult projects, but chores that will take you, step by step, toward your rainbow. Write them down, if you must, but limit your list so that you won't have to drag today's undone matters into tomorrow. Remember that you cannot build your pyramid in twenty-four hours. Be patient. Never allow your day to become so cluttered that you neglect your most important goal—to do the best you can, enjoy this day, and rest satisfied with what you have accomplished."
—*Og Mandino*

48. "To desire is to obtain; to aspire is to achieve."
—*James Allen*

49. "Winners take time to relish their work, knowing that scaling the mountain is what makes the view from the top so exhilarating."
—*Denis Waitley*

50. "Great things are not done by impulse, but by a series of small things brought together."
—*Vincent Van Gogh*

51. "The person with a fixed goal, a clear picture of his desire, or an ideal always before him, causes it, through repetition, to be buried deeply in his subconscious mind and is thus enabled, thanks to its generative and sustaining power, to realize his goal in a minimum of time and with a minimum of physical effort. Just pursue the thought unceasingly. Step by step you will achieve realization, for all your faculties and powers become directed to that end."
—*Claude M. Bristol*

52. "If you wish to achieve worthwhile things in your personal and career life, you must become a worthwhile person in your own self-development."
—*Brian Tracy*

53. "To focus on technique is like cramming your way through school. You sometimes get by, perhaps even get good grades, but if you don't pay the price day in and day out, you'll never achieve true mastery of the subjects you study or develop an educated mind."
—*Stephen R. Covey*

54. "If you can imagine it, you can achieve it; if you can dream it, you can become it."
—*William Arthur Ward*

55. "What a great discrepancy there is between men and the results they achieve! It is due to the difference in their power of calling together all the rays of their ability, and concentrating them upon one point."
—*Orison Swett Marden*

56. "Nothing stops the man who desires to achieve. Every obstacle is simply a course to develop his achievement muscle. It's a strengthening of his powers of accomplishment."
—*Eric Butterworth*

57. "Not the maker of plans and promises, but rather the one who offers faithful service in small matters. This is the person who is most likely to achieve what is good and lasting."
—*Johann Wolfgang von Goethe*

ACTION

58. "Knowing is not enough; we must apply. Willing is not enough; we must do."
—*Johann Wolfgang von Goethe*

59. "When I stand before God at the end of my life, I would hope that I would not have a single bit of talent left, and could say, "I used everything you gave me.""
—*Erma Bombeck*

60. "Thinking is easy, acting is difficult, and to put one's thoughts into action is the most difficult thing in the world."
—*Johann Wolfgang von Goethe*

61. "You have to be before you can do, and do before you can have."
—*Zig Ziglar*

62. "It is not the critic who counts; not the man who points out how the strong man stumbles, or where the doer of deeds could have done them better. The credit belongs to the man who is actually in the arena, whose face is marred by dust and sweat and blood, who strives valiantly; who errs and comes short again and again; because there is not effort without error and shortcomings; but who does actually strive to do the deed; who knows the great enthusiasm, the great devotion, who spends himself in a worthy cause, who at the best knows in the end the triumph of high achievement and who at the worst, if he fails, at least he fails while daring greatly. So that his place shall never be with those cold and timid souls who know neither victory nor defeat."
    —*Theodore Roosevelt*

63. "I have been impressed with the urgency of doing. Knowing is not enough; we must apply. Being willing is not enough; we must do."
    —*Leonardo da Vinci*

64. "Don't wait. The time will never be just right."
    —*Napoleon Hill*

65. "The more you are willing to accept responsibility for your actions, the more credibility you will have."
    —*Brian Koslow*

66. "I never worry about action, but only about inaction."
    —*Winston Churchill*

67. "Believe and act as if it were impossible to fail."
    —*Charles F. Kettering*

68. "Everything you want is out there waiting for you to ask. Everything you want also wants you. But you have to take action to get it."
    —*Jules Renard*

69. "Action is the real measure of intelligence."
—*Napoleon Hill*

70. "The possibilities are numerous once we decide to act and not react."
—*George Bernard Shaw*

71. "It is not only what we do, but also what we do not do, for which we are accountable."
—*Moliere*

72. "Your actions, and your action alone, determines your worth."
—*Johann G. Fichte*

73. "To map out a course of action and follow it to an end requires courage."
—*Ralph Waldo Emerson*

74. "Great acts are made up of small deeds."
—*Lao Tzu*

75. "The path to success is to take massive, determined action."
—*Anthony Robbins*

76. "Beings are owners of their action, heirs of their action."
—*Buddha*

77. "You see, in life, lots of people know what to do, but few people actually do what they know. Knowing is not enough! You must take action."
—*Anthony Robbins*

78. "Motivation is what gets you started. Habit is what keeps you going."
—*Jim Rohn*

79. "Risk! Risk anything! Care no more for the opinions of others, for those voices. Do the hardest thing on earth for you. Act for yourself. Face the truth."
    —*Katherine Mansfield*

80. "The self is not something ready-made, but something in continuous formation through choice of action."
    —*John Dewey*

81. "Whatever you do may seem insignificant, but it is most important that you do it."
    —*Mahatma Gandhi*

82. "You may never know what results come of your action, but if you do nothing there will be no result."
    —*Mahatma Gandhi*

83. "Often the difference between a successful person and a failure is not one has better abilities or ideas, but the courage that one has to bet on one's ideas, to take a calculated risk—and to act."
    —*Andre Malraux*

84. "The only cure for grief is action."
    —*G. H. Lewes*

85. "Success seems to be connected with action. Successful people keep moving. They make mistakes, but they don't quit."
    —*Conrad Hilton*

86. "Behave so the aroma of your actions may enhance the general sweetness of the atmosphere."
    —*Henry David Thoreau*

87. "We become just by performing just actions, temperate by performing temperate actions, brave by performing brave actions."
    —*Aristotle*

88. "Action may not always bring happiness; but there is no happiness without action."
—*Benjamin Disraeli*

89. "Words may show a man's wit, but actions his meaning."
—*Benjamin Franklin*

90. "As I grow older, I pay less attention to what people say. I just watch what they do."
—*Andrew Carnegie*

91. "As you begin changing your thinking, start immediately to change your behaviour. Begin to act the part of the person you would like to become. Take action on your behaviour. Too many people want to feel, then take action. This never works."
—*John Maxwell*

92. "Action may not bring happiness but there is no happiness without action."
—*William James*

93. "Thoughts lead on to purpose, purpose leads on to actions, actions form habits, habits decide character, and character fixes our destiny."
—*Tryon Edwards*

94. "It's the little things you do that can make a big difference. What are you attempting to accomplish? What little thing can you do today that will make you more effective? You are probably only one step away from greatness."
—*Bob Proctor*

95. "High achievers spot rich opportunities swiftly, make big decisions quickly and move into action immediately. Follow these principles and you can make your dreams come true."
—*Robert H. Schuller*

ATTITUDE

96. "Seek out that particular mental attribute which makes you feel most deeply and vitally alive, along with which comes the inner voice which says, 'This is the real me,' and when you have found that attitude, follow it."
—*William James*

97. "Any fact facing us is not as important as our attitude toward it, for that determines our success or failure. The way you think about a fact may defeat you before you ever do anything about it. You are overcome by the fact because you think you are."
—*Norman Vincent Peale*

98. "I think there is something, more important than believing: Action! The world is full of dreamers, there aren't enough who will move ahead and begin to take concrete steps to actualize their vision."
—*W. Clement Stone*

99. "Ability is what you're capable of doing. Motivation determines what you do. Attitude determines how well you do it."
—*Lou Holtz*

100. "You cannot control what happens to you, but you can control your attitude toward what happens to you, and in that, you will be mastering change rather than allowing it to master you."
—*Brian Tracy*

101. "Attitude is a little thing that makes a big difference."
—*Winston Churchill*

102. "Your attitude, not your aptitude, will determine your altitude."
—*Zig Ziglar*

103. "The meaning of things lies not in the things themselves, but in our attitude towards them."
—*Antoine de Saint-Exupery*

104. "Our attitude toward life determines life's attitude towards us."
—*John N. Mitchell*

105. "Any fact facing us is not as important as our attitude toward it, for that determines our success or failure."
—*Norman Vincent Peale*

106. "We cannot change our past. We can not change the fact that people act in a certain way. We can not change the inevitable. The only thing we can do is play on the one string we have, and that is our attitude."
—*Charles R. Swindoll*

107. "If you think you can do it, you can. If you believe you can do it, you will. If you trust you can do it, you will make a difference."
—*Catherine Ellis*

108. "Happiness doesn't depend on any external conditions, it is governed by our mental attitude."
—*Dale Carnegie*

109. "The one thing you can't take away from me is the way I choose to respond to what you do to me. The last of one's freedoms is to choose ones attitude in any given circumstance."
—*Viktor Frankl*

110. "Attitudes are nothing more than habits of thoughts, and habits can be acquired. An action repeated becomes an attitude realized."
—*Paul Myer*

111. "Your living is determined not so much by what life brings to you as by the attitude you bring to life; not so much by what happens to you as by the way your mind looks at what happens."
—*Kahlil Gibran*

112. "Whenever you're in conflict with someone, there is one factor that can make the difference between damaging your relationship and deepening it. That factor is attitude."
—*William James*

113. "There is little difference in people, but that little difference makes a big difference. The little difference is attitude. The big difference is whether it is positive or negative."
—*W. Clement Stone*

114. "Attitude is more important than the past, than education, than money, than circumstances, than what people do or say. It is more important than appearance, giftedness, or skill."
—*W. C. Fields*

115. "Nothing can stop the man with the right mental attitude from achieving his goal; nothing on earth can help the man with the wrong mental attitude."
—*Thomas Jefferson*

116. "If you don't like something, change it. If you can't change it, change your attitude."
—*Maya Angelou*

117. "I believe the single most significant decision I can make on a day-to-day basis is my choice of attitude. It is more important than my past, my education, my bankroll, my successes or failures, fame or pain, what other people think of me or say about me, my circumstances, or my position. Attitude keeps me going or cripples my progress. It alone fuels my fire or assaults my hope. When my attitudes are right, there is no barrier too high, no valley too deep, no dream too extreme, no challenge too great for me."
—*Charles R. Swindoll*

118. "A positive attitude may not solve every problem but it makes solving any problem a more pleasant experience."
—*Grant Fairley*

119. "It is our attitude at the beginning of a difficult undertaking which, more than anything else, will determine its successful outcome."
—*William James*

120. "For success, attitude is equally as important as ability."
—*Harry F. Banks*

121. "A conviction of self-worth and passion for ideals fuse in a life attitude that is positive, free, noble and spiritually enhancing."
—*Bill Jay*

122. "It is very important to generate a good attitude, a good heart, as much as possible. From this, happiness in both the short term and the long term for both yourself and others will come."
—*Dalai Lama*

123. "Excellence is not a skill. It is an attitude."
—*Ralph Marston*

CHANGE

124. "If there is anything that we wish to change in the child, we should first examine it and see whether it is not something that could better be changed in ourselves."
—*Carl Jung*

125. "Action and reaction, ebb and flow, trial and error, change—this is the rhythm of living. Out of our over-confidence, fear; out of our fear, clearer vision, fresh hope. And out of hope, progress."
—*Bruce Barton*

126. "All changes, even the most longed for, have their melancholy; for what we leave behind us is a part of ourselves; we must die to one life before we can enter another."
—*Anatole France*

127. "Always remember that the future comes one day at a time."
—*Dean Acheson*

128. "Any change, even a change for the better, is always accompanied by drawbacks and discomforts."
—*Arnold Bennett*

129. "He that will not apply new remedies must expect new evils; for time is the greatest innovator."
—*Francis Bacon*

130. "He who rejects change is the architect of decay. The only human institution which rejects progress is the cemetery."
—*Harold Wilson*

131. "If there is no struggle, there is no progress."
—*Frederick Douglass*

132. "Change always comes bearing gifts."
—*Price Pritchett*

133. "It is not the strongest of the species that survive, nor the most intelligent, the the one most responsive to change."
—*Charles Darwin*

134. "It's the most unhappy people who most fear change."
—*Mignon McLaughlin*

135. "If we don't change, we don't grow. If we don't grow, we aren't really living."
—*Gail Sheehy*

136. "Life belongs to the living, and he who lives must be prepared for changes."
—*Johann Wolfgang von Goethe*

137. "The world hates change, yet it is the only thing that has brought progress."
—*Charles Kettering*

138. "They must often change, who would be constant in happiness or wisdom."
—*Confucius*

139. "Things alter for the worse spontaneously, if they be not altered for the better designedly."
—*Francis Bacon*

140. "Things do not change; we change."
—*Henry David Thoreau*

141. "Without change, something sleeps inside us, and seldom awakens. The sleeper must awaken."
—*Frank Herbert*

142. "If you don't like something change it; if you can't change it, change the way you think about it."
—*Mary Engelbreit*

143. "When we are no longer able to change a situation, we are challenged to change ourselves."
—*Victor Frankl*

144. "The only difference between a rut and a grave is their dimensions."
—*Ellen Glasgow*

145. "Growth is the only evidence of life."
—*John Henry Newman*

146. "Time is a dressmaker specializing in alterations."
—*Faith Baldwin*

147. "The circumstances of the world are so variable that an irrevocable purpose or opinion is almost synonymous with a foolish one."
—*William H. Seward*

148. "The birds are molting. If only man could molt also—his mind once a year its errors, his heart once a year its useless passions."
—*James Allen*

149. "The man who never alters his opinion is like standing water, and breeds reptiles of the mind."
—*William Blake*

150. "What you have become is the price you paid to get what you used to want."
—*Mignon McLaughlin*

151. "Those who expect moments of change to be comfortable and free of conflict have not learned their history."
—*Joan Wallach Scott*

152. "After you've done a thing the same way for two years, look it over carefully. After five years, look at it with suspicion. And after ten years, throw it away and start all over."
—*Alfred Edward Perlman*

153. "If you would attain to what you are not yet, you must always be displeased by what you are. For where you are pleased with yourself there you have remained. Keep adding, keep walking, keep advancing."
—*Saint Augustine*

154. "Continuity gives us roots; change gives us branches, letting us stretch and grow and reach new heights."
—*Pauline R. Kezer*

155. "A good question is never answered. It is not a bolt to be tightened into place but a seed to be planted and to bear more seed toward the hope of greening the landscape of idea."
—*John Ciardi*

156. "Every beginning is a consequence—every beginning ends some thing."
—*Paul Valery*

157. "God grant me the serenity to accept the people I cannot change, the courage to change the one I can, and the wisdom to know it's me."
—*Unknown*

158. "Neither a wise man nor a brave man lies down on the tracks of history to wait for the train of the future to run over him."
—*Dwight D. Eisenhower*

159. "The only man I know who behaves sensibly is my tailor; he takes my measurements anew each time he sees me. The rest go on with their old measurements and expect me to fit them."
—*George Bernard Shaw*

CHOICE

160. "Every human has four endowments—self awareness, conscience, independent will and creative imagination. These give us the ultimate human freedom... The power to choose, to respond, to change."
—*Stephen R. Covey*

161. "It's choice--not chance--that determines your destiny."
—*Jean Nidetch*

162. "By choosing not to allow parts of ourselves to exist, we are forced to expend huge amounts of psychic energy to keep them beneath the surface."
—*Debbie Ford*

163. "Your life is the sum result of all the choices you make, both consciously and unconsciously. If you can control the process of choosing, you can take control of all aspects of your life. You can find the freedom that comes from being in charge of yourself."
—*Robert F. Bennett*

164. "There is a point at which everything becomes simple and there is no longer any question of choice, because all you have staked will be lost if you look back. Life's point of no return."
—*Dag Hammarskjold*

165. "Be miserable. Or motivate yourself. Whatever has to be done, it's always your choice."
—*Wayne Dyer*

166. "Choose your love, Love your choice."
—*Thomas S. Monson*

167. "Every choice moves us closer to or farther away from something. Where are your choices taking your life? What do your behaviors demonstrate that you are saying yes or no to in life?"
—*Eric Allenbaugh*

168. "There are three constants in life... change, choice and principles."
—*Stephen R. Covey*

169. "Man is unique in that he has plans, purpose and goals which require the need for criteria of choice. The need for ethical value is within man whose future may largely be determined by the choice he make."
—*George Bernard Shaw*

170. "Every man builds his world in his own image. He has the power to choose, but no power to escape the necessity of choice."
—*Ayn Rand*

171. "When you have to make a choice and don't make it, that is in itself a choice."
—*William James*

172. "Every choice you make has an end result."
—*Zig Ziglar*

173. "The remarkable thing is, we have a choice everyday regarding the attitude we will embrace for that day."
—*Charles R. Swindoll*

174. "The strongest principle of growth lies in human choice."
—*George Eliot*

175. "The self is not something ready-made, but something in continuous formation through choice of action."
—*John Dewey*

176. "Destiny is no matter of chance. It is a matter of choice: It is not a thing to be waited for, it is a thing to be achieved."
—*William Jennings Bryan*

177. "We choose what attitudes we have right now. And it's a continuing choice."
—*John Maxwell*

178. "You and I are essentially infinite choice-makers. In every moment of our existence, we are in that field of all possibilities where we have access to an infinity of choices."
—*Deepak Chopra*

179. "It is always your next move."
—*Napoleon Hill*

180. "It is your own convictions which compels you; that is, choice compels choice."
—*Epictetus*

CONFIDENCE

181. "People who ask confidently get more than those who are hesitant and uncertain. When you've figured out what you want to ask for, do it with certainty, boldness and confidence."
—*Jack Canfield*

182. "The greatest waste in the world is the difference between what we are and what we could become."
—*Ben Herbster*

183. "Your past is not your potential. In any hour you can choose to liberate the future."
—*Marilyn Ferguson*

184. "Questions provide the key to unlocking our unlimited potential."
—*Anthony Robbins*

185. "We all have possibilities we don't know about. We can do things we don't even dream we can do."
—*Dale Carnegie*

186. "Our society nurtures the illusion that all the rewards go to the people who are perfect. But many of us are finding out that trying to be perfect is costly."
—*Debbie Ford*

187. "I was always looking outside myself for strength and confidence but it comes from within. It is there all the time."
—*Anna Freud*

188. "Everything you need you already have. You are complete right now, you are a whole, total person, not an apprentice person on the way to someplace else. Your completeness must be understood by you and experienced in your thoughts as your own personal reality."
—*Wayne Dyer*

189. "Confidence comes not from always being right but from not fearing to be wrong."
—*Peter T. Mcintyre*

190. "The man of genius inspires us with a boundless confidence in our own powers."
—*Ralph Waldo Emerson*

191. "Count your blessings. Once you realize how valuable you are and how much you have going for you, the smiles will return, the sun will break out, the music will play, and you will finally be able to move forward the life that God intended for you with grace, strength, courage, and confidence."
—*Og Mandino*

192. "Don't back down just to keep the peace. Standing up for your beliefs builds self-confidence and self-esteem."
—*Oprah Winfrey*

193. "Life is not easy for any of us. But what of that? We must have perseverance and above all confidence in ourselves. We must believe that we are gifted for something, and that this thing, at whatever cost, must be attained."
—*Marie Curie*

194. "All you need in this life is ignorance and confidence, and then success is sure."
—*Mark Twain*

195. "Confidence is going after Moby Dick in a rowboat and taking the tartar sauce with you."
—*Zig Ziglar*

196. "Experience tells you what to do; confidence allows you to do it."
—*Stan Smith*

197. "To succeed in life, you need two things: ignorance and confidence."
—*Mark Twain*

198. "Who has confidence in himself will gain the confidence of others."
—*Leib Lazarow*

199. "Whatever we expect with confidence becomes our own self-fulfilling prophecy."
—*Brian Tracy*

200. "With realization of one's own potential and self-confidence in one's ability, one can build a better world."
—*Dalai Lama*

201. "As soon as you trust yourself, you will know how to live."
—*Johann Wolfgang von Goethe*

202. "When you're a beautiful person on the inside, there is nothing in the world that can change that about you. Jealousy is the result of one's lack of self-confidence, self-worth, and self-acceptance. The Lesson: If you can't accept yourself, then certainly no one else will."
—*Sasha Azevedo*

203. "If you have no confidence in self, you are twice defeated in the race of life. With confidence, you have won even before you have started."
—*Marcus Tullius Cicero*

204. "One important key to success is self-confidence. An important key to self-confidence is preparation."
—*Arthur Ashe*

205. "Confidence is contagious; so is lack of confidence."
—*Vince Lombardi*

206. "Guts are a combination of confidence, courage, conviction, strength of character, stick-to-itiveness, pugnaciousness, backbone, and intestinal fortitude. They are mandatory for anyone who wants to get to and stay at the top."
—*D. A. Benton*

207. "Nothing builds self-esteem and self-confidence like accomplishment."
—*Thomas Carlyle*

208. "The history of the world is full of men who rose to leadership, by sheer force of self-confidence, bravery and tenacity."
—*Mahatma Gandhi*

209. "There can be no failure to a man who has not lost his courage, his character, his self respect, or his self-confidence. He is still a King."
—*Orison Swett Marden*

210. "Confidence is that feeling by which the mind embarks in great and honorable courses with a sure hope and trust in itself."
—*Marcus Tullius Cicero*

211. "Self-confidence is the first requisite to great undertakings."
—*Samuel Johnson*

212. "As is our confidence, so is our capacity."
—*William Hazlitt*

213. "Confidence... thrives on honesty, on honor, on the sacredness of obligations, on faithful protection and on unselfish performance. Without them it cannot live."
—*Franklin D. Roosevelt*

214. "If I have lost confidence in myself, I have the universe against me."
—*Ralph Waldo Emerson*

215. "Health is the greatest possession. Contentment is the greatest treasure. Confidence is the greatest friend. Non-being is the greatest joy."
—*Lao Tzu*

DECISION

216. "It's in your moments of decision that your destiny is shaped."
—*Anthony Robbins*

217. "Everything is something you decide to do, and there is nothing you have to do."
—*Denis Waitley*

218. "It doesn't matter which side of the fence you get off on sometimes. What matters most is getting off. You cannot make progess without making decisions."
—*Jim Rohn*

219. "The possibilities are numerous once we decide to act and not react."
—*George Bernard Shaw*

220. "Each player must accept the cards life deals him or her: but once they are in hand, he or she alone must decide how to play the cards in order to win the game."
—*Voltaire*

221. "Decide that you want it more than you are afraid of it."
—*Bill Cosby*

222. "Build this day on a foundation of pleasant thoughts. Never fret at any imperfections that you fear may impede your progress. Remind yourself, as often as necessary, that you are a creature of God and have the power to achieve any dream by lifting up your thoughts. You can fly when you decide that you can. Never consider yourself defeated again. Let the vision in your heart be in your life's blueprint. Smile!"
—*Og Mandino*

223. "You are the person who has to decide. Whether you'll do it or toss it aside; You are the person who makes up your mind. Whether you'll lead or will linger behind. Whether you'll try for the goal that's afar. Or just be contented to stay where you are."
—*Edgar A. Guest*

224. "The only person you are destined to become is the person you decide to be."
—*Ralph Waldo Emerson*

225. "Whatever course you decide upon, there is always someone to tell you that you are wrong. There are always difficulties arising which tempt you to believe that your critics are right. To map out a course of action and follow it to an end requires courage."
—*Ralph Waldo Emerson*

226. "Nothing is more difficult, and therefore more precious, than to be able to decide."
—*Napoleon Bonaparte*

227. "The happiest people are those who think the most interesting thoughts. Those who decide to use leisure as a means of mental development, who love good music, good books, good pictures, good company, good conversation, are the happiest people in the world. And they are not only happy in themselves, they are the cause of happiness in others."
—*William Lyon Phelps*

228. "Each of you, for himself, by himself and on his own responsibility, must speak. And it is a solemn and weighty responsibility, and not lightly to be flung aside at the bullying of pulpit, press, government, or the empty catchphrases of politicians. Each must for himself alone decide what is right and what is wrong, and which course is patriotic and which isn't. You cannot shirk this and be a man. To decide against your convictions is to be an unqualified and inexcusable traitor, both to yourself and to your country, let man label you as they may. If you alone of all the nation shall decide one way, and that way be the right way according to your convictions of the right, you have done your duty by yourself and by your country— hold up your head! You have nothing to be ashamed of."
—*Mark Twain*

229. "When we least expect it, life sets us a challenge to test our courage and willingness to change; at such a moment, there is no point in pretending that nothing has happened or in saying that we are not ready. The challenge will not wait. Life does not look back. A week is more than enough time for us to decide whether or not to accept our destiny."
—*Paulo Coelho*

230. "You can't ask for what you want unless you know what it is. A lot of people don't know what they want or they want much less than they deserve. First you have figure out what you want. Second, you have to decide that you deserve it. Third, you have to believe you can get it. And, fourth, you have to have the guts to ask for it."
—*Barbara De Angelis*

231. "The best day of your life is the one on which you decide your life is your own. No apologies or excuses. No one to lean on, rely on, or blame. The gift is yours—it is an amazing journey—and you alone are responsible for the quality of it. This is the day your life really begins."
—*Bob Moawad*

232. "There are two ways of being happy: We must either diminish our wants or augment our means—either may do—the result is the same and it is for each man to decide for himself and to do that which happens to be easier."
—*Benjamin Franklin*

233. "There Is A Voice Inside Of You, That Whispers All Day Long, "I Feel That This Is Right For Me, I Know That This Is Wrong." No Teacher, Preacher, Parent, Friend Or Wise Man Can Decide What's Right For You—Just Listen To The Voice That Speaks Inside.""
—*Shel Silverstein*

234. "Our ultimate freedom is the right and power to decide how anybody or anything outside ourselves will affect us."
—*Stephen R. Covey*

235. "Decide what you want, decide what you are willing to exchange for it. Establish your priorities and go to work."
—*H. L. Hunt*

236. "You are always a valuable, worthwhile human being—not because anybody says so, not because you're successful, not because you make a lot of money—but because you decide to believe it and for no other reason."
—*Wayne Dyer*

237. "Every noble work is bound to face problems and obstacles. It is important to check your goal and motivation thoroughly. One should be very truthful, honest, and reasonable. One's actions should be good for others, and for oneself as well. Once a positive goal is chosen, you should decide to pursue it all the way to the end. Even if it is not realized, at least there will be no regret."
—*Dalai Lama*

238. "Every man must decide whether he will walk in the light of creative altruism or in the darkness of destructive selfishness."
—*Martin Luther King, Jr.*

239. "You have brains in your head. You have feet in your shoes. You can steer yourself in any direction you choose. You're on your own. And you know what you know. You are the guy who'll decide where to go."
—*Dr. Seuss*

240. "Our power is in our ability to decide."
—*Richard Buckminster Fuller*

241. "I've continued to recognize the power individuals have to change virtually anything and everything in their lives in an instant. I've learned that the resources we need to turn our dreams into reality are within us, merely waiting for the day when we decide to wake up and claim our birthright."
—*Anthony Robbins*

242. "It does not take much strength to do things, but it requires great strength to decide on what to do."
—*Elbert Hubbard*

243. "If your head tells you one thing, and your heart tells you another, before you do anything, you should first decide whether you have a better head or a better heart."
—*Marilyn vos Savant*

244. "Keep true, never be ashamed of doing right; decide on what you think is right and stick to it."
—*T.S. Eliot*

245. "If you raise your children to feel that they can accomplish any goal or task they decide upon, you will have succeeded as a parent and you will have given your children the greatest of all blessings."
—*Brian Tracy*

246. "Man is a being with free will; therefore, each man is potentially good or evil, and it's up to him and only him (through his reasoning mind) to decide which he wants to be."
—*Ayn Rand*

247. "The day you decide to do it is your lucky day."
—*Japanese Proverb*

248. "Everything starts with yourself / with you making up your mind about what you're going to do with your life. I tell kids that it's a cruel world, and that the world will bend them either left or right, and it's up to them to decide which way to bend."
—*Tony Dorsett*

249. "Every man gotta right to decide his own destiny."
—*Bob Marley*

250. "The most difficult thing is the decision to act, the rest is merely tenacity. The fears are paper tigers. You can do anything you decide to do. You can act to change and control your life; and the procedure , the process is its own reward."
—*Amelia Earhart*

DESIRE

251. "The only place where your dream becomes impossible is in your own thinking."
—*Robert H. Schuller*

252. "Dream no small dreams for they have no power to move the hearts of men."
—*Goethe*

253. "Out of need springs desire, and out of desire springs the energy and the will to win."
—*Denis Waitley*

254. "Without a sense of urgency, desire loses its value."
—*Jim Rohn*

255. "Desire is the starting point of all achievement, not a hope, not a wish, but a keen pulsating desire which transcends everything."
—*Napoleon Hill*

256. "Your hopes, dreams and aspirations are legitimate. They are trying to take you airborne, above the clouds, above the storms, if you only let them."
—*William James*

257. "The first principle of success is desire—knowing what you want. Desire is the planting of your seed."
—*Robert Collier*

258. "There is one quality which one must possess to win, and that is definiteness of purpose, the knowledge of what one wants, and a burning desire to possess it."
—*Napoleon Hill*

259. "You can have anything you want—if you want it badly enough. You can be anything you want to be, do anything you set out to accomplish if you hold to that desire with singleness of purpose."
—*Abraham Lincoln*

260. "The starting point of all achievement is desire."
—*Napoleon Hill*

261. "Whatever you vividly imagine, ardently desire, sincerely believe, and enthusiastically act upon must inevitably come to pass."
—*Paul J. Meyer*

262. "Human behavior flows from three main sources: desire, emotion, and knowledge."
—*Plato*

263. "Reduce your plan to writing. The moment you complete this, you will have definitely given concrete form to the intangible desire."
—*Napoleon Hill*

264. "Plant the seed of desire in your mind and it forms a nucleus with power to attract to itself everything needed for its fulfillment."
—*Robert Collier*

265. "Create a definite plan for carrying out your desire and begin at once, whether you ready or not, to put this plan into action."
—*Napoleon Hill*

266. "The key to success is to focus our conscious mind on things we desire not things we fear."
—*Brian Tracy*

267. "The more you seek security, the less of it you have. But the more you seek opportunity, the more likely it is that you will achieve the security that you desire."
—*Brian Tracy*

268. "The desire of gold is not for gold. It is for the means of freedom and benefit."
—*Ralph Waldo Emerson*

269. "Thoughts mixed with definiteness of purpose, persistence, and a burning desire are powerful things."
—*Napoleon Hill*

270. "There is a desire deep within the soul which drives man from the seen to the unseen, to philosophy and to the divine."
—*Kahlil Gibran*

271. "Boredom: the desire for desires."
—*Leo Nikolaevich Tolstoy*

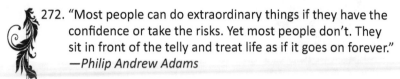

272. "Most people can do extraordinary things if they have the confidence or take the risks. Yet most people don't. They sit in front of the telly and treat life as if it goes on forever."
—*Philip Andrew Adams*

273. "A creative man is motivated by the desire to achieve, not by the desire to beat others."
—*Ayn Rand*

274. "To desire and strive to be of some service to the world, to aim at doing something which shall really increase the happiness and welfare and virtue of mankind—this is a choice which is possible for all of us; and surely it is a good haven to sail for."
—*Henry Van Dyke*

275. "Imagination is the beginning of creation. You imagine what you desire, you will what you imagine and at last you create what you will."
—*George Bernard Shaw*

276. "Burning desire to be or do something gives us staying power—a reason to get up every morning or to pick ourselves up and start in again after a disappointment."
—*Marsha Sinetar*

277. "When you discover your mission, you will feel its demand. It will fill you with enthusiasm and a burning desire to get to work on it."
—*W. Clement Stone*

278. "One great question underlies our experience, whether we think about it or not: what is the purpose of life? From the moment of birth every human being wants happiness and does not want suffering. Neither social conditioning nor education nor ideology affects this. From the very core of our being, we simply desire contentment. Therefore, it is important to discover what will bring about the greatest degree of happiness."
—*Dalai Lama*

279. "If you greatly desire something, have the guts to stake everything on obtaining it."
—*Brendan Francis*

280. "You will become as small as your controlling desire; as great as your dominant aspiration."
—*James Allen*

281. "Those who desire to give up freedom in order to gain security will not have, nor do they deserve, either one."
—*Benjamin Franklin*

282. "When you love people and have the desire to make a profound, positive impact upon the world, then will you have accomplished the meaning to live."
—*Sasha Azevedo*

283. "The desire is thy prayers; and if thy desire is without ceasing, thy prayer will also be without ceasing. The continuance of your longing is the continuance of your prayer."
—*Saint Augustine*

284. "Everything is perfect in the universe—even your desire to improve it."
—*Wayne Dyer*

285. "It is for us to pray not for tasks equal to our powers, but for powers equal to our tasks, to go forward with a great desire forever beating at the door of our hearts as we travel toward our distant goal."
—*Helen Keller*

286. "One of the most difficult things everyone has to learn is that for your entire life you must keep fighting and adjusting if you hope to survive. No matter who you are or what your position is you must keep fighting for whatever it is you desire to achieve."
—*George Allen*

287. "Happiness can be defined, in part at least, as the fruit of the desire and ability to sacrifice what we want now for what we want eventually."
—*Stephen R. Covey*

288. "The will to win, the desire to succeed, the urge to reach your full potential... these are the keys that will unlock the door to personal excellence."
—*Confucius*

289. "Image creates desire. You will what you imagine."
—*J. G. Gallimore*

DREAMS

290. "Believe in your dreams and they may come true; believe in yourself and they will come true."
—*Unknown*

291. "Consult not your fears but your hopes and your dreams. Think not about your frustrations, but about your unfulfilled potential. Concern yourself not with what you tried and failed in, but with what it is still possible for you to do."
—*Pope John XXIII*

292. "Happy are those who dream dreams and are ready to pay the price to make them come true."
—*Leon Joseph Cardinal Suenens*

293. "We grow by our dreams."
—*Woodrow T. Wilson*

294. "There is hope in dreams, imagination, and in the courage of those who wish to make those dreams a reality."
—*Jonas Salk*

295. "Dreams are illustrations... from the book your soul is writing about you."
—*Marsha Norman*

296. "Cherish your visions and your dreams as they are the children of your soul; the blueprints of your ultimate achievements."
—*Napoleon Hill*

297. "We all have our time machines. Some take us back, they're called memories. Some take us forward, they're called dreams."
—*Jeremy Irons*

298. "Dreams do come true, if we only wish hard enough.You can have anything in life if you will sacrifice everything else for it."
—*James Matthew Barrie*

299. "The only thing that will stop you from fulfilling your dreams is you."
—*Tom Bradley*

300. "Dreams are today's answers to tomorrow's questions."
—*Edgar Cayce*

301. "If one advances confidently in the direction of one's dreams, and endeavors to live the life which one has imagined, one will meet with a success unexpected in common hours."
—*Henry David Thoreau*

302. "Somewhere over the rainbow, skies are blue, and the dreams that you dare to dream really do come true."
—*Lyman Frank Baum*

303. "Trust in dreams, for in them is hidden the gate to eternity."
—*Kahlil Gibran*

304. "Your vision will become clear only when you look into your heart. Who looks outside, dreams. Who looks inside, awakens."
—*Carl Gustav Jung*

305. "Be careful what you water your dreams with. Water them with worry and fear and you will produce weeds that choke the life from your dream. Water them with optimism and solutions and you will cultivate success. Always be on the lookout for ways to turn a problem into an opportunity for success. Always be on the lookout for ways to nurture your dream."
—*Lao Tzu*

306. "You're in the midst of a war: a battle between the limits of a crowd seeking the surrender of your dreams, and the power of your true vision to create and contribute. It is a fight between those who will tell you what you cannot do, and that part of you that knows / and has always known / that we are more than our environment; and that a dream, backed by an unrelenting will to attain it, is truly a reality with an imminent arrival."
—*Anthony Robbins*

307. "The victory of success is half won when one gains the habit of setting goals and achieving them. Even the most tedious chore will become endurable as you parade through each day convinced that every task, no matter how menial or boring, brings you closer to fulfilling your dreams."
—*Og Mandino*

308. "Dreams and dedication are a powerful combination."
—*William Longgood*

309. "I prefer to be a dreamer among the humblest, with visions to be realized, than lord among those without dreams and desires."
—*Kahlil Gibran*

310. "We dance for laughter, we dance for tears, we dance for madness, we dance for fears, we dance for hopes, we dance for screams, we are the dancers, we create the dreams."
    —*Unknown*

311. "You have to dream before your dreams can come true."
    —*Abdul Kalam*

312. "Even the wildest dreams have to start somewhere. Allow yourself the time and space to let your mind wander and your imagination fly."
    —*Oprah Winfrey*

313. "The best reason for having dreams is that in dreams no reasons are necessary."
    —*Ashleigh Brilliant*

314. "I believe that imagination is stronger than knowledge—myth is more potent than history—dreams are more powerful than facts—hope always triumphs over experience—laughter is the cure for grief—love is stronger than death."
    —*Robert Fulghum*

315. "Dreams pass into the reality of action. From the actions stems the dream again; and this interdependence produces the highest form of living."
    —*Anais Nin*

316. "A fool dreams of wealth; a wise man, of happiness."
    —*Turkish Proverb*

FAITH

317. "If you can conceive it in your mind, then it can be brought to the physical world."
—*Bob Proctor*

318. "Faith is not belief without proof, but trust without reservation."
—*Unknown*

319. "Faith... is the art of holding on to things your reason once accepted, despite your changing moods."
—*C.S. Lewis*

320. "When you have come to the edge of all light that you know and are about to drop off into the darkness Of the unknown, Faith is knowing One of two things will happen: There will be something solid to stand on or You will be taught to fly."
—*Patrick Overton*

321. "Everything you are seeking are seeking you in return. Therefore, everything you want is already yours. So, you don't have to get anything. It is simply a matter of becoming more aware of what you already possess."
—*Bob Proctor*

322. "The reason birds can fly and we can't is simply that they have perfect faith, for to have faith is to have wings."
—*James Matthew Barrie*

323. "You block your dream when you allow your fear to grow bigger than your faith."
—*Mary Manin Morrissey*

324. "To one who has faith, no explanation is necessary. To one without faith, no explanation is possible."
—*St. Thomas Aquinas*

325. "Thoughts become things. If you see it in your mind, you will hold it in your hand."
—*Bob Proctor*

326. "Faith consists in believing when it is beyond the power of reason to believe."
—*Voltaire*

327. "Just as the body cannot exist without blood, so the soul needs the matchless and pure strength of faith."
—*Mahatma Gandhi*

328. "The only thing that stands between a man and what he wants from life is often merely the will to try it and the faith to believe that it is possible."
—*David Viscott*

329. "The man who cannot believe in himself cannot believe in anything else. The basis of all integrity and character is whatever faith we have in our own integrity."
—*Roy L. Smith*

330. "The only limits in our life are those we impose on ourselves."
—*Bob Proctor*

331. "The smallest seed of faith is better than the largest fruit of happiness."
—*Henry David Thoreau*

332. "Scepticism is the beginning of Faith."
—*Oscar Wilde*

333. "If you can envision it, you can have it!."
—*Bob Proctor*

334. "I do believe that when we face challenges in life that are far beyond our own power, it's an opportunity to build on our faith, inner strength, and courage. I've learned that how we face challenges plays a big role in the outcome of them."
—*Sasha Azevedo*

335. "Each of us has an inner dream that we can unfold if we will just have the courage to admit what it is. And the faith to trust our own admission. The admitting is often very difficult."
—*Julia Cameron*

336. "Faith is to believe what you do not see; the reward of this faith is to see what you believe."
—*Saint Augustine*

337. "Faith is a knowledge within the heart, beyond the reach of proof."
—*Kahlil Gibran*

338. "As your faith is strengthened you will find that there is no longer the need to have a sense of control, that things will flow as they will, and that you will flow with them, to your great delight and benefit."
—*Emmanuel Teney*

339. "Faith is a process of leaping into the abyss not on the basis of any certainty about ~where~ we shall land, but rather on the belief that we ~shall~ land."
—*Carter Heyward*

340. "Faith sees a beautiful blossom in a bulb, a lovely garden in a seed, and a giant oak in an acorn."
—*William Arthur Ward*

341. "Faith is not something to grasp, it is a state to grow into."
—*Mahatma Gandhi*

342. "Painting is a faith, and it imposes the duty to disregard public opinion."
—*Vincent van Gogh*

343. "A faith to live by, a self to live with, and a purpose to live for."
—*Bob Harrington*

344. "Faith is taking the first step even when you don't see the whole staircase."
—*Martin Luther King, Jr.*

345. "Faith is not belief. Belief is passive. Faith is active."
—*Edith Hamilton*

346. "Faith is the daring of the soul to go farther than it can see."
—*William Newton Clarke*

347. "The foundation stones for a balanced success are honesty, character, integrity, faith, love and loyalty."
—*Zig Ziglar*

348. "A faith is a necessity to a man. Woe to him who believes in nothing."
—*Victor Hugo*

349. "There is but one cause of human failure. And that is man's lack of faith in his true Self."
—*William James*

350. "In faith there is enough light for those who want to believe and enough shadows to blind those who don't."
—*Blaise Pascal*

351. "There are nine requisites for contented living: HEALTH enough to make work a pleasure; WEALTH enough to support your needs; STRENGTH enough to battle with difficulties and forsake them; GRACE enough to confess your sins and overcome them; PATIENCE enough to toil until some good is accomplished; CHARITY enough to see some good in your neighbor; LOVE enough to move you to be useful and helpful to others; FAITH enough to make real the things of God; HOPE enough to remove all anxious fears concerning the future."
   —*Johann Wolfgang von Goethe*

352. "Faith is the confidence, the assurance, the enforcing truth, the knowing."
   —*Robert Collier*

353. "On a long journey of human life, faith is the best of companions; it is the best refreshment on the journey; and it is the greatest property."
   —*Buddha*

354. "Faith makes the discords of the present the harmonies of the future."
   —*Robert Collyer*

355. "All of the great achievers of the past have been visionary figures; they were men and women who projected into the future. They thought of what could be, rather than what already was, and then they moved themselves into action, to bring these things into fruition."
   —*Bob Proctor*

356. "When you really want something, and you couple that with an understanding of your nature, of your spiritual being, and the laws that govern you, you will keep going, regardless of what's happened. Nothing will stop you."
   —*Bob Proctor*

357. "To believe in the things you can see and touch is no belief at all. But to believe in the unseen is both a triumph and a blessing."
—*Bob Proctor*

358. "You have to believe it's possible and believe in yourself. Because after you've decided what you want, you have to believe it's possible, and possible for you, not just for other people. Then you need to seek out models, mentors, and coaches."
—*Jack Canfield*

359. "On a long journey of human life, faith is the best of companions; it is the best refreshment on the journey; and it is the greatest property."
—*Buddha*

360. "There are laws of the universe and if you practice them they will respond to you."
—*Michael Beckwith*

361. "The most valuable things in life are not measured in monetary terms. The really important things are not houses and lands, stocks and bonds, automobiles and real estate, but friendships, trust, confidence, empathy, mercy, love and faith."
—*Bertrand Russell*

362. "Believe in yourself! Have faith in your abilities! Without a humble but reasonable confidence in your own powers you cannot be successful or happy."
—*Norman Vincent Peale*

363. "The real source of wealth and capital in this new era is not material things... it is the human mind, the human spirit, the human imagination, and our faith in the future."
—*Steve Forbes*

364. "Every achiever that I have ever met says, 'My life turned around when I began to believe in me.'"
—*Dr. Robert H. Schuller*

FEAR

365. "Most fears cannot withstand the test of careful scrutiny and analysis. When we expose our fears to the light of thoughtful examination they usually just evaporate."
—Jack Canfield

366. "You block your dream when you allow your fear to grow bigger than your faith."
—*Mary Manin Morrissey*

367. "Let fear be a counselor and not a jailer."
—*Anthony Robbins*

368. "Fear less, hope more; Eat less, chew more; Whine less, breathe more; Talk less, say more; Love more, and all good things will be yours."
—*Swedish Proverb*

369. "Ultimately we know deeply that the other side of every fear is freedom."
—*Marilyn Ferguson*

370. "The whole secret of existence is to have no fear. Never fear what will become of you, depend on no one. Only the moment you reject all help are you freed."
—*Buddha*

371. "The wise man in the storm prays to God, not for safety from danger, but deliverance from fear."
—*Ralph Waldo Emerson*

372. "Courage is resistance to fear, mastery of fear—not
     absence of fear."
     —*Mark Twain*

373. "To overcome a fear, here's all you have to do: realize the
     fear is there, and do the action you fear anyway."
     —*Peter McWilliams*

374. "Procrastination is the fear of success. People procrastinate
     because they are afraid of the success that they know
     will result if they move ahead now. Because success is
     heavy, carries a responsibility with it, it is much easier to
     procrastinate and live on the 'someday I'll' philosophy."
     —*Denis Waitley*

375. "You can conquer almost any fear if you will only make
     up your mind to do so. For remember, fear doesn't exist
     anywhere except in the mind."
     —*Dale Carnegie*

376. "Fear is the main source of superstition, and one of the
     main sources of cruelty. To conquer fear is the beginning of
     wisdom."
     —*Bertrand Russell*

377. "Do what you fear, and the death of fear is certain."
     —*Anthony Robbins*

378. "He who fears to suffer, suffers from fear."
     —*French Proverb*

379. "Do the thing you fear to do and keep on doing it... that is
     the quickest and surest way ever yet discovered to conquer
     fear."
     —*Dale Carnegie*

380. "Inaction breeds doubt and fear. Action breeds confidence
     and courage. If you want to conquer fear, do not sit home
     and think about it. Go out and get busy."
     —*Dale Carnegie*

381. "He who is not everyday conquering some fear has not learned the secret of life."
—*Ralph Waldo Emerson*

382. "If you look into your own heart, and you find nothing wrong there, what is there to worry about? What is there to fear?"
—*Confucius*

383. "Fear is something to be moved through, not something to be turned from."
—*Peter McWilliams*

384. "FEAR is an acronym in the English language for 'False Evidence Appearing Real.'"
—*Neale Donald Walsch*

385. "Fear is a habit; so is self-pity, defeat, anxiety, despair, hopelessness and resignation. You can eliminate all of these negative habits with two simple resolves: I can!! and I will!!."
—*Unknown*

386. "You gain strength, courage, and confidence by every experience in which you really stop to look fear in the face... do the thing you think you cannot do."
—*Eleanor Roosevelt*

387. "Do what you fear most and you control fear."
—*Tom Hopkins*

388. "Courage leads to heaven; fear to death."
—*Seneca*

389. "There are four ways you can handle fear. You can go over it, under it, or around it. But if you are ever to put fear behind you, you must walk straight through it. Once you put fear behind you, leave it there."
—*Donna A. Favors*

390. "Courage is not the absence of fear, but rather the judgement that something else is more important than fear."
—*Ambrose Redmoon*

391. "Our deepest fear is not that we are inadequate. Our deepest fear is that we are powerful beyond measure. It is our light, not our darkness, that most frightens us. We ask ourselves, who am I to be brilliant, gorgeous, talented, and fabulous? Actually, who are you not to be? You are a child of God. Your playing small doesn't serve the world. There's nothing enlightened about shrinking so that other people won't feel insecure around you. We are all meant to shine, as children do. We are born to make manifest the glory of God that is within us. It's not just in some of us, it's in everyone. And as we let our own light shine, we unconsciously give other people permission to do the same. As we are liberated from our own fear, our presence automatically liberates others."
—*Marianne Williamson*

392. "I must not fear. Fear is the mind-killer. Fear is the little-death that brings total obliteration. I will face my fear... And when it is gone past I will turn the inner eye to see its path. Where the fear is gone there will be nothing. Only I will remain."
—*Frank Herbert*

393. "Since fear is mostly about ignorance, the best part is that it's as temporary as you choose."
—*Christine Comaford*

394. "The world we see that seems so insane is the result of a belief system that is not working. To perceive the world differently, we must be willing to change our belief system, let the past slip away, expand our sense of now, and dissolve the fear in our minds."
—*William James*

395. "I have often been afraid, but I wouldn't give in to it. I made myself act as though I was not afraid, and gradually my fear disappeared."
—*Theodore Roosevelt*

396. "Listen to what you know instead of what you fear."
—*Richard Bach*

397. "Worry is a thin stream of fear trickling through the mind. If encouraged, it cuts a channel into which all other thoughts are drained."
—*Arthur Somers Roche*

398. "Fear an ignorant man more than a lion."
—*Turkish Proverb*

399. "They who have conquered doubt and fear have conquered failure."
—*James Allen*

400. "Normal fear protects us; abnormal fear paralyses us. Normal fear motivates us to improve our individual and collective welfare; abnormal fear constantly poisons and distorts our inner lives. Our problem is not to be rid of fear but, rather to harness and master it."
—*Martin Luther King, Jr.*

401. "Indecision is the seedling of fear."
—*Napoleon Hill*

FOCUS

402. "It's not what's happening to you now or what has happened in your past that determines who you become. Rather, it's your decisions about what to focus on, what things mean to you, and what you're going to do about them that will determine your ultimate destiny."
—*Anthony Robbins*

403. "It is wise to direct your anger towards problems—not people; to focus your energies on answers—not excuses."
—*William Arthur Ward*

404. "When you write down your ideas you automatically focus your full attention on them. Few if any of us can write one thought and think another at the same time. Thus a pencil and paper make excellent concentration tools."
—*Michael Leboeuf*

405. "One reason so few of us achieve what we truly want is that we never direct our focus; we never concentrate our power. Most people dabble their way through life, never deciding to master anything in particular."
—*Anthony Robbins*

406. "Goals provide the energy source that powers our lives. One of the best ways we can get the most from the energy we have is to focus it. That is what goals can do for us; concentrate our energy."
—*Denis Waitley*

407. "Don't dwell on what went wrong. Instead, focus on what to do next. Spend your energies on moving forward toward finding the answer."
—*Denis Waitley*

408. "Goals are a means to an end, not the ultimate purpose of our lives. They are simply a tool to concentrate our focus and move us in a direction. The only reason we really pursue goals is to cause ourselves to expand and grow. Achieving goals by themselves will never make us happy in the long term; it's who you become, as you overcome the obstacles necessary to achieve your goals, that can give you the deepest and most long-lasting sense of fulfillment."
—*Anthony Robbins*

409. "Most people have no idea of the giant capacity we can immediately command when we focus all of our resources on mastering a single area of our lives."
—*Anthony Robbins*

410. "Focus on your potential instead of your limitations."
—*Alan Loy McGinnis*

411. "You can't depend on your judgment when your imagination is out of focus."
—*Mark Twain*

412. "Life is a train of moods like a string of beads; and as we pass through them they prove to be many colored lenses, which paint the world their own hue, and each shows us only what lies in its own focus."
—*Ralph Waldo Emerson*

413. "It is during our darkest moments that we must focus to see the light."
—*Aristotle Onassis*

414. "Focus more on your desire than on your doubt, and the dream will take care of itself. You may be surprised at how easily this happens. Your doubts are not as powerful as your desires, unless you make them so."
—*Marcia Wieder*

415. "I find hope in the darkest of days, and focus in the brightest. I do not judge the universe."
—*Dalai Lama*

416. "All blame is a waste of time. No matter how much fault you find with another, and regardless of how much you blame him, it will not change you. The only thing blame does is to keep the focus off you when you are looking for external reasons to explain your unhappiness or frustration. You may succeed in making another feel guilty about something by blaming him, but you won't succeed in changing whatever it is about you that is making you unhappy."
—*Wayne Dyer*

417. "Most people have no idea of the giant capacity we can immediately command when we focus all of our resources on mastering a single area of our lives."
—*Anthony Robbins*

418. "You can't depend on your eyes when your imagination is out of focus."
—*Mark Twain*

419. "Focus 90% of your time on solutions and only 10% of your time on problems."
—*Anthony J. D'Angelo*

420. "Rather than denying problems, focus inventively, intentionally on what solutions might look or feel like... Our mind is meant to generate ideas that help us escape circumstantial traps / if we trust it to do so. Naturally, not all hunches are useful. But then you only need a single good idea to solve a problem."
—*Marsha Sinetar*

421. "Focus on the journey, not the destination. Joy is found not in finishing an activity but in doing it."
—*Greg Anderson*

422. "Your future takes precedence over your past. Focus on your future, rather than on the past."
—*Gary Ryan Blair*

423. "If you want to be truly successful invest in yourself to get the knowledge you need to find your unique factor. When you find it and focus on it and persevere your success will blossom."
—*Sidney Madwed*

424. "Lose not yourself in a far off time, seize the moment that is thine."
—*Johann Friedrich Von Schiller*

425. "Both abundance and lack exist simultaneously in our lives, as parallel realities. It is always our conscious choice which secret garden we will tend... when we choose not to focus on what is missing from our lives but are grateful for the abundance that's present / love, health, family, friends, work, the joys of nature and personal pursuits that bring us pleasure / the wasteland of illusion falls away and we experience Heaven on earth."
—*Sarah Ban Breathnach*

426. "Concentrate all your thoughts upon the work at hand. The sun's rays do not burn until brought to a focus."
—*Alexander Graham Bell*

427. "A mind at peace, a mind centered and not focused on harming others, is stronger than any physical force in the universe."
—*Wayne Dyer*

428. "When I chased after money, I never had enough. When I got my life on purpose and focused on giving of myself and everything that arrived into my life, then I was prosperous."
—*Wayne Dyer*

429. "Only when your consciousness is totally focused on the moment you are in can you receive whatever gift, lesson, or delight that moment has to offer."
—*Barbara De Angelis*

430. "When every physical and mental resources is focused, one's power to solve a problem multiplies tremendously."
—*Norman Vincent Peale*

431. "Productivity is never an accident. It is always the result of a commitment to excellence, intelligent planning, and focused effort."
—*Paul J. Meyer*

432. "You must remain focused on your journey to greatness."
—*Les Brown*

FORGIVENESS

433. "Resentment is like taking poison and waiting for the other person to die."
—*Malachy McCourt*

434. "Forgiveness is not always easy. At times, it feels more painful than the wound we suffered, to forgive the one that inflicted it. And yet, there is no peace without forgiveness."
—*Marianne Williamson*

435. "The past is over and done and cannot be changed. This is the only moment we can experience."
—*Louise Hay*

436. "Whatever we refuse to recognize about ourselves has a way of rearing its head and making itself known when we least expect it."
—*Debbie Ford*

437. "I really don't think life is about the I-could-have-beens. Life is only about the I-tried-to-do. I don't mind the failure but I can't imagine that I'd forgive myself if I didn't try."
—*Nikki Giovanni*

438. "To understand everything is to forgive everything."
—*Buddha*

439. "To love means loving the unlovable. To forgive means pardoning the unpardonable. Faith means believing the unbelievable. Hope means hoping when everything seems hopeless."
—*G. K. Chesterton*

440. "Love yourself—accept yourself—forgive yourself—and be good to yourself, because without you the rest of us are without a source of many wonderful things."
—*Leo F. Buscaglia*

441. "Flatter me, and I may not believe you. Criticize me, and I may not like you. Ignore me, and I may not forgive you. Encourage me, and I will not forget you. Love me and I may be forced to love you."
—*William Arthur Ward*

442. "To forgive is to set a prisoner free and discover that the prisoner was you."
—*Lewis B. Smedes*

443. "Before you speak, listen. Before you write, think. Before you spend, earn. Before you invest, investigate. Before you criticize, wait. Before you pray, forgive. Before you quit, try. Before you retire, save. Before you die, give."
—*William Arthur Ward*

444. "Sincere forgiveness isn't colored with expectations that the other person apologize or change. Don't worry whether or not they finally understand you. Love them and release them. Life feeds back truth to people in its own way and time."
—*Sara Paddison*

445. "When a deep injury is done us, we never recover until we forgive."
—*Alan Paton*

446. "Do more than belong: participate. Do more than care: help. Do more than believe: practice. Do more than be fair: be kind. Do more than forgive: forget. Do more than dream: work."
—*William Arthur Ward*

447. "Forgive yourself for your faults and your mistakes and move on."
—*Les Brown*

448. "Let us forgive each other—only then will we live in peace."
—*Leo Nikolaevich Tolstoy*

449. "Forgiveness does not change the past, but it does enlarge the future."
—*Paul Boese*

450. "The weak can never forgive. Forgiveness is the attribute of the strong."
—*Mahatma Gandhi*

451. "Without forgiveness life is governed by an endless cycle of resentment and retaliation."
—*Roberto Assagioli*

452. "Friendship flourishes at the fountain of forgiveness."
—*William Arthur Ward*

453. "Forgiveness is the key that unlocks the door of resentment and the handcuffs of hate. It is a power that breaks the chains of bitterness and the shackles of selfishness."
—*William Arthur Ward*

454. "The best thing to give to your enemy is forgiveness; to an opponent, tolerance; to a friend, your heart; to your child, a good example; to a father, deference; to your mother, conduct that will make her proud of you; to yourself, respect; to all men, charity."
—*Benjamin Franklin*

455. "True forgiveness is not an action after the fact, it is an attitude with which you enter each moment."
—*David Ridge*

456. "We achieve inner health only through forgiveness—the forgiveness not only of others but also of ourselves."
—*Joshua Loth Liebman*

457. "Inner peace can be reached only when we practice forgiveness. Forgiveness is letting go of the past, and is therefore the means for correcting our misperceptions."
—*Gerald Jampolsky*

458. "Forgiveness is the economy of the heart... forgiveness saves the expense of anger, the cost of hatred, the waste of spirits."
—*Hannah Moore*

459. "Forgiveness is the giving, and so the receiving, of life."
—*George MacDonald*

FRIENDSHIP

460. "A friend is one of the nicest things you can have, and one of the best things you can be."
—*Douglas Pagels*

461. "Friendship isn't a big thing—it's a million little things."
—*Unknown*

462. "A single rose can be my garden... a single friend, my world."
—*Leo Buscaglia*

463. "Only your real friends will tell you when your face is dirty."
—*Sicilian Proverb*

464. "The antidote for fifty enemies is one friend."
—*Aristotle*

465. "In everyone's life, at some time, our inner fire goes out. It is then burst into flame by an encounter with another human being. We should all be thankful for those people who rekindle the inner spirit."
—*Albert Schweitzer*

466. "A loyal friend laughs at your jokes when they're not so good, and sympathizes with your problems when they're not so bad."
—*Arnold H. Glasgow*

467. "The friend is the man who knows all about you, and still likes you."
—*Elbert Hubbard*

468. "The most I can do for my friend is simply be his friend."
—*Henry David Thoreau*

469. "A true friend never gets in your way unless you happen to be going down."
    —*Arnold Glasow*

470. "But if the while I think on thee, dear friend, all losses are restored and sorrows end."
    —*William Shakespeare*

471. "The most beautiful discovery true friends make is that they can grow separately without growing apart."
    —*Elisabeth Foley*

472. "A friend knows the song in my heart and sings it to me when my memory fails."
    —*Donna Roberts*

473. "You can always tell a real friend: when you've made a fool of yourself he doesn't feel you've done a permanent job."
    —*Laurence J. Peter*

474. "If a friend is in trouble, don't annoy him by asking if there is anything you can do. Think up something appropriate and do it."
    —*Edgar Watson Howe*

475. "Friends are those rare people who ask how you are and then wait for the answer."
    —*Unknown*

476. "A friend is the one who comes in when the whole world has gone out."
    —*Grace Pulpit*

477. "Constant use will not wear ragged the fabric of friendship."
    —*Dorothy Parker*

478. "The best kind of friend is the one you could sit on a porch with, never saying a word, and walk away feeling like that was the best conversation you've had."
—*Unknown*

479. "The language of friendship is not words but meanings."
—*Henry David Thoreau*

480. "A true friend is one who thinks you are a good egg even if you are half-cracked."
—*Unknown*

481. "If instead of a gem, or even a flower, we should cast the gift of a loving thought into the heart of a friend, that would be giving as the angels give."
—*George MacDonald*

482. "It takes a long time to grow an old friend."
—*John Leonard*

483. "He who has a thousand friends has not a friend to spare, and he who has one enemy will meet him everywhere."
—*Ralph Waldo Emerson*

484. "We are keenly aware of the faults of our friends, but if they like us enough it doesn't matter."
—*Mignon McLaughlin*

485. "A true friend unbosoms freely, advises justly, assists readily, adventures boldly, takes all patiently, defends courageously, and continues a friend unchangeably."
—*William Penn*

486. "A good friend is a connection to life—a tie to the past, a road to the future, the key to sanity in a totally insane world."
—*Lois Wyse*

487. "If you're alone, I'll be your shadow. If you want to cry, I'll be your shoulder. If you want a hug, I'll be your pillow. If you need to be happy, I'll be your smile. But anytime you need a friend, I'll just be me."
—*Unknown*

488. "A man's growth is seen in the successive choirs of his friends."
—*Ralph Waldo Emerson*

GOALS

489. "Set a goal to achieve something that is so big, so exhilarating that it excites you and scares you at the same time. It must be a goal that is so appealing, so much in line with your spiritual core, that you can't get it out of your mind. If you do not get chills when you set a goal, you're not setting big enough goals."
—*Bob Proctor*

490. "Not in his goals but in his transitions is man great."
—*Ralph Waldo Emerson*

491. "Discipline is the bridge between goals and accomplishment."
—*Jim Rohn*

492. "If you know what to do to reach your goal, it's not a big enough goal."
—*Bob Proctor*

493. "Setting goals is the first step in turning the invisible into the visible."
—*Anthony Robbins*

494. "The most important key to achieving great success is to decide upon your goal and launch, get started, take action, move."
—*Brian Tracy*

495. "People are not lazy. They simply have impotent goals / that is, goals that do not inspire them."
—*Anthony Robbins*

496. "We come this way but once. We can either tiptoe through life and hope we get to death without being badly bruised or we can live a full, complete life achieving our goals and realizing our wildest dreams."
—*Bob Proctor*

497. "Without goals, and plans to reach them, you are like a ship that has set sail with no destination."
—*Fitzhugh Dodson*

498. "Goals are dreams with deadlines."
—*Diana Scharf Hunt*

499. "When it is obvious that the goals cannot be reached, don't adjust the goals, adjust the action steps."
—*Confucius*

500. "Your purpose explains what you are doing with your life. Your vision explains how you are living your purpose. Your goals enable you to realize your vision."
—*Bob Proctor*

501. "Learn from the past, set vivid, detailed goals for the future, and live in the only moment of time over which you have any control: now."
—*Denis Waitley*

502. "In the absence of clearly-defined goals, we become strangely loyal to performing daily trivia until ultimately we become enslaved by it."
—*Robert Heinlein*

503. "The reason most people never reach their goals is that they don't define them, learn about them, or even seriously consider them as believable or achievable. Winners can tell you where they are going, what they plan to do along the way, and who will be sharing the adventure with them."
—*Denis Waitley*

504. "All who have accomplished great things have had a great aim; have fixed their gaze on a goal which was high, one which sometimes seemed impossible."
—*Orison Swett Marden*

505. "Setting goals is the first step in turning the invisible into the visible."
—*Anthony Robbins*

506. "The reason most people never reach their goals is that they don't define them, learn about them, or even seriously consider them as believable or achievable. Winners can tell you where they are going, what they plan to do along the way, and who will."
—*Denis Waitley*

507. "When you are clear, what you want will show up in your life, and only to the extent you are clear."
—*Janet Attwood*

508. "To have Goals is to have a future, because without goals we will strive for nothing."
—*Andrew Ridings*

509. "Goals provide the energy source that powers our lives. One of the best ways we can get the most from the energy we have is to focus it. That is what goals can do for us; concentrate our energy."
—*Denis Waitley*

510. "Know your goal, make a plan and pull the trigger."
—*Phil C. McGraw*

511. "Man is a goal seeking animal. His life only has meaning if he is reaching out and striving for his goals."
—*Aristotle*

512. "Goals allow you to control the direction of change in your favor."
—*Brian Tracy*

513. "Our goals can only be reached through a vehicle of a plan, in which we must fervently believe, and upon which we must vigorously act. There is no other route to success."
—*Stephen A. Brennan*

514. "You must take action now that will move you towards your goals. Develop a sense of urgency in your life."
—*H. Jackson Brown, Jr.*

515. "The most important thing you can do to achieve your goals is to make sure that as soon as you set them, you immediately begin to create momentum. The most important rules that I ever adopted to help me in achieving my goals were those I learned from a very successful man who taught me to first write down the goal, and then to never leave the site of setting a goal without firs taking some form of positive action toward its attainment."
—*Anthony Robbins*

516. "People with goals succeed because they know where they're going."
—*Earl Nightingale*

517. "Whenever you make a mistake or get knocked down by life, don't look back at it too long. Mistakes are life's way of teaching you. Your capacity for occasional blunders is inseparable from your capacity to reach your goals. No one wins them all, and your failures, when they happen, are just part of your growth. Shake off your blunders. How will you know your limits without an occasional failure? Never quit. Your turn will come."
—*Og Mandino*

518. "Anything inside that immobilizes me, gets in my way, keeps me from my goals, is all mine."
—*Wayne Dyer*

519. "When your goals seem too difficult to reach... move the posts closer."
—*Phil Long*

520. "What you get by achieving your goals is to as important as what you become by achieving your goals."
—*Zig Ziglar*

521. "Your goals are the road maps that guide you and show you what is possible for your life."
—*Les Brown*

522. "If I feel depressed I will sing. If I feel sad I will laugh. If I feel ill I will double my labor. If I feel fear I will plunge ahead. If I feel inferior I will wear new garments. If I feel uncertain I will raise my voice. If I feel poverty I will think of wealth to come. If I feel incompetent I will think of past success. If I feel insignificant I will remember my goals. Today I will be the master of my emotions."
—*Og Mandino*

523. "Every single life only becomes great when the individual sets upon a goal or goals which they really believe in, which they can really commit themselves to, which they can put their whole heart and soul into."
—*Brian Tracy*

524. "Goals are not only absolutely necessary to motivate us. They are essential to really keep us alive."
—*Robert H. Schuller*

525. "The most important thing about having goals is having one."
—*Abert F. Geoffrey*

526. "You must see your goals clearly and specifically before you

can set out for them. Hold them in your mind until they
become second nature."
—*Les Brown*

527. "Don't be a time manager, be a priority manager. Cut your
major goals into bite-sized pieces. Each small priority or
requirement on the way to ultimate goal become a mini
goal in itself."
—*Denis Waitley*

528. "Far away there in the sunshine are my highest aspirations.
I may not reach them, but I can look up and see their
beauty, believe in them, and try to follow there they lead."
—*Louisa May Alcott*

529. "If you're bored with life—you don't get up every morning
with a burning desire to do things—you don't have enough
goals."
—*Lou Holtz*

530. "We are built to conquer environment, solve problems,
achieve goals, and we find no real satisfaction or happiness
in life without obstacles to conquer and goals to achieve."
—*Maxwell Maltz*

531. "A person should set his goals as early as he can and
devote all his energy and talent to getting there. With
enough effort, he may achieve it. Or he may find something
that is even more rewarding. But in the end, no matter
what the outcome, he will know he has been alive."
—*Walt Disney*

GRATITUDE

532. "Let's start with what we can be thankful for, and get our mind into that vibration, and then watch the good that starts to come, because one thought leads to another thought."
—*Bob Proctor*

533. "Two kinds of gratitude: the sudden kind we feel for what we take; the larger kind we feel for what we give."
—*Edwin Arlington Robinson*

534. "Let us be grateful to people who make us happy, they are the charming gardeners who make our souls blossom."
—*Marcel Proust*

535. "Gratitude makes sense of our past, brings peace for today, and creates a vision for tomorrow."
—*Unknown*

536. "The enlightened give thanks for what most people take for granted... As you begin to be grateful for what most people take for granted, that vibration of gratitude makes you more receptive to good in your life."
—*Michael Beckwith*

537. "Gratitude is an attitude that hooks us up to our source of supply. And the more grateful you are, the closer you become to your maker, to the architect of the universe, to the spiritual core of your being. It's a phenomenal lesson."
—*Bob Proctor*

538. "Gratitude unlocks the fullness of life. It turns what we have into enough, and more. It turns denial into acceptance, chaos to order, confusion to clarity. It can turn a meal into a feast, a house into a home, a stranger into a friend. Gratitude makes sense of our past, brings peace for today, and creates a vision for tomorrow."
—*Melody Beattie*

539. "At times our own light goes out and is rekindled by a spark from another person. Each of us has cause to think with deep gratitude of those who have lighted the flame within us."
—*Albert Schweitzer*

540. "When you are grateful, fear disappears and abundance appears."
—*Anthony Robbins*

541. "Develop an attitude of gratitude, and give thanks for everything that happens to you, knowing that every step forward is a step toward achieving something bigger and better than your current situation."
—*Brian Tracy*

542. "I would maintain that thanks are the highest form of thought, and that gratitude is happiness doubled by wonder."
—*G. K. Chesterton*

543. "When it comes to life the critical thing is whether you take things for granted or take them with gratitude."
—*G. K. Chesterton*

544. "Feeling gratitude and not expressing it is like wrapping a present and not giving it."
—*William Arthur Ward*

545. "As we express our gratitude, we must never forget that the highest appreciation is not to utter words, but to live by them."
—*John Fitzgerald Kennedy*

546. "Gratitude is when memory is stored in the heart and not in the mind."
—*Lionel Hampton*

547. "No one who achieves success does so without acknowledging the help of others. The wise and confident acknowledge this help with gratitude."
—*Alfred North Whitehead*

548. "I have learned that some of the nicest people you'll ever meet are those who have suffered a traumatic event or loss. I admire them for their strength, but most especially for their life gratitude—a gift often taken for granted by the average person in society."
—*Sasha Azevedo*

549. "Good men and bad men differ radically. Bad men never appreciate kindness shown them, but wise men appreciate and are grateful. Wise men try to express their appreciation and gratitude by some return of kindness, not only to their benefactor, but to e."
—*Buddha*

550. "Gratitude bestows reverence, allowing us to encounter everyday epiphanies, those transcendent moments of awe that change forever how we experience life and the world."
—*John Milton*

551. "Gratitude is a duty which ought to be paid, but which none have a right to expect."
—*Jean-Jacques Rousseau*

552. "God gave you a gift of 86,400 seconds today. Have you used one to say 'thank you?'"
—*William Arthur Ward*

553. "If the only prayer you said in your whole life was, 'thank you,' that would suffice."
—*Meister Eckhart*

554. "The only people with whom you should try to get even are those who have helped you."
—*John E. Southard*

555. "As each day comes to us refreshed and anew, so does my gratitude renew itself daily. The breaking of the sun over the horizon is my grateful heart dawning upon a blessed world."
—*Terri Guillemets*

556. "For each new morning with its light, For rest and shelter of the night, For health and food, for love and friends, For everything Thy goodness sends."
—*Ralph Waldo Emerson*

557. "The unthankful heart... discovers no mercies; but let the thankful heart sweep through the day and, as the magnet finds the iron, so it will find, in every hour, some heavenly blessings!."
—*Henry Ward Beecher*

558. "He is a wise man who does not grieve for the things which he has not, but rejoices for those which he has."
—*Epictetus*

559. "Not what we say about our blessings, but how we use them, is the true measure of our thanksgiving."
—*W.T. Purkiser*

560. "Gratitude is a quality similar to electricity: it must be produced and discharged and used up in order to exist at all."
—*William Faulkner*

561. "If you want to turn your life around, try thankfulness. It will change your life mightily."
—*Gerald Good*

562. "The hardest arithmetic to master is that which enables us to count our blessings."
—*Eric Hoffer*

HAPPINESS

563. "Don't look back on happiness or dream of it in the future. You are only sure of today; do not let yourself be cheated out of it."
—*Henry Ward Beecher*

564. "It is not easy to find happiness in ourselves, and it is not possible to find it elsewhere."
—*Agnes Repplier*

565. "Finally, what I really want is to be happy in this moment, where the magic and miracles happen. Stay in the moment and all gifts are added as you breathe and take inspired action."
—*Joe Vitale*

566. "Man is fond of counting his troubles, but he does not count his joys. If he counted them up as he ought to, he would see that every lot has enough happiness provided for it."
—*Fyodor Dostoevsky*

567. "If you want to be happy, set a goal that commands your thoughts, liberates your energy and inspires your hopes."
—*Andrew Carnegie*

568. "If you want to be happy, be."
—*Leo Tolstoy*

569. "Most people would rather be certain they're miserable, than risk being happy."
—*Robert Anthony*

570. "The best way to cheer yourself up is to try to cheer somebody else up."
—*Mark Twain*

571. "Nobody really cares if you're miserable, so you might as well be happy."
—*Cynthia Nelms*

572. "Those who can laugh without cause have either found the true meaning of happiness or have gone stark raving mad."
—*Norm Papernick*

573. "What a wonderful life I've had! I only wish I'd realized it sooner."
—*Colette*

574. "The foolish man seeks happiness in the distance; the wise grows it under his feet."
—*James Openheim*

575. "People take different roads seeking fulfillment and happiness. Just because they're not on your road doesn't mean they've gotten lost."
—*H. Jackson Browne*

576. "Happiness is like a butterfly which, when pursued, is always beyond our grasp, but, if you will sit down quietly, may alight upon you."
—*Nathaniel Hawthorne*

577. "Often people attempt to live their lives backwards; they try to have more things, or more money, in order to do more of what they want, so they will be happier. The way it actually works is the reverse. You must first be who you really are, then do what you need to do, in order to have what you want."
—*Margaret Young*

578. "It's never too late to have a happy childhood."
—*Berke Breathed*

579. "Happiness? That's nothing more than health and a poor memory."
—*Albert Schweitzer*

580. "If you want others to be happy, practice compassion. If you want to be happy, practice compassion."
—*Dalai Lama*

581. "Happiness held is the seed; happiness shared is the flower."
—*Unknown*

582. "He is rich or poor according to what he is, not according to what he has."
—*Henry Ward Beecher*

583. "If you search the world for happiness, you may find it in the end, for the world is round and will lead you back to your door."
—*Robert Brault*

584. "Cheerfulness is what greases the axles of the world. Don't go through life creaking."
—*H.W. Byles*

585. "For every minute you are angry you lose sixty seconds of happiness."
—*Ralph Waldo Emerson*

586. "It is not easy to find happiness in ourselves, and it is not possible to find it elsewhere."
—*Agnes Repplier*

587. "Happiness equals reality minus expectations."
—*Tom Magliozzi*

588. "The greatest happiness of life is the conviction that we are loved—loved for ourselves, or rather, loved in spite of ourselves."
—*Victor Hugo*

589. "There is only one way to happiness and that is to cease worrying about things which are beyond the power of our will."
—*Epictetus*

590. "This very moment is a seed from which the flowers of tomorrow's happiness grow."
—*Margaret Lindsey*

591. "Get happiness out of your work or you may never know what happiness is."
—*Elbert Hubbard*

592. "It is not in doing what you like, but in liking what you do that is the secret of happiness."
—*James Matthew Barrie*

593. "Happiness comes of the capacity to feel deeply, to enjoy simply, to think freely, to risk life, to be needed."
—*Storm Jameson*

594. "Happiness is not something ready made. It comes from your own actions."
—*Dalai Lama*

595. "Happiness is when what you think, what you say, and what you do are in harmony."
—*Mohandas Gandhi*

596. "Success in its highest and noblest form calls for peace of mind and enjoyment and happiness which come only to the man who has found the work that he likes best."
—*Napoleon Hill*

597. "Happiness is not a goal; it is a by-product."
—*Eleanor Roosevelt*

598. "True happiness... is not attained through self-gratification, but through fidelity to a worthy purpose."
—*Helen Keller*

599. "Are you bored with life? Then throw yourself into some work you believe in with all your heart, live for it, die for it, and you will find happiness that you had thought could never be yours."
—*Dale Carnegie*

600. "Happiness is not something you postpone for the future; it is something you design for the present."
—*Jim Rohn*

601. "But what is happiness except the simple harmony between a man and the life he leads?"
—*Albert Camus*

602. "There is no value in life except what you choose to place upon it and no happiness in any place except what you bring to it yourself."
—*Henry David Thoreau*

603. "The happiness of your life depends upon the quality of your thoughts: therefore, guard accordingly, and take care that you entertain no notions unsuitable to virtue and reasonable nature."
—*Marcus Aurelius*

604. "Happiness is a continuation of happenings which are not resisted."
—*Deepak Chopra*

605. "Happiness makes up in height for what it lacks in length."
—*Robert Frost*

606. "The person born with a talent they are meant to use will find their greatest happiness in using it."
—*Johann Wolfgang von Goethe*

607. "There is a difference between happiness and wisdom: he that thinks himself the happiest man is really so; but he that thinks himself the wisest is generally the greatest fool."
—*Francis Bacon*

608. "The happiness of a man in this life does not consist in the absence but in the mastery of his passions."
—*Alfred Lord Tennyson*

609. "Happiness cannot be traveled to, owned, earned, worn or consumed. Happiness is the spiritual experience of living every minute with love, grace, and gratitude."
—*Denis Waitley*

610. "A man is not rightly conditioned until he is a happy, healthy, and prosperous being; and happiness, health, and prosperity are the result of a harmonious adjustment of the inner with the outer of the man with his surroundings."
—*James Allen*

HOPE

611. "In all things it is better to hope than to despair."
—*Johann Wolfgang von Goethe*

612. "Hope never abandons you; you abandon it."
—*George Weinberg*

613. "Hope is the companion of power, and mother of success; for who so hopes strongly has within him the gift of miracles."
—*Samuel Smiles*

614. "Hope works in these ways: it looks for the good in people instead of harping on the worst; it discovers what can be done instead of grumbling about what cannot; it regards problems, large or small, as opportunities; it pushes ahead when it would be easy to quit; it 'lights the candle' instead of 'cursing the darkness.'"
—*Anonymous*

615. "What seems to us as bitter trials are often blessings in disguise."
—*Oscar Wilde*

616. "Learn from yesterday, live for today, hope for tomorrow."
—*Albert Einstein*

617. "Hope is faith holding out its hand in the dark."
—*George Iles*

618. "What oxygen is to the lungs, such is hope to the meaning of life."
—*Emil Brunner*

619. "Hope is the thing with feathers, that perches in the soul, and sings the tune without words, and never stops at all."
—*Emily Dickinson*

620. "Most of the important things in the world have been accomplished by people who have kept on trying when there seemed to be no hope at all."
—*Dale Carnegie*

621. "What would life be if we had no courage to attempt anything?"
—*Vincent van Gogh*

622. "Hope arouses, as nothing else can arouse, a passion for the possible."
—*William Sloan Coffin*

623. "The very least you can do in your life is to figure out what you hope for. And the most you can do is live inside that hope."
—*Barbara Kingsolver*

624. "Once you choose hope, anything's possible."
—*Christopher Reeve*

625. "When the world says, 'Give up,' Hope whispers, 'Try it one more time.'"
—*Unknown*

626. "The road that is built in hope is more pleasant to the traveler than the road built in despair, even though they both lead to the same destination."
—*Marian Zimmer Bradley*

627. "Hope is the word which God has written on the brow of every man."
—*Victor Hugo*

IMAGINATION

628. "Only as high as I reach can I grow, only as far as I seek can I go, only as deep as I look can I see, only as much as I dream can I be."
—*Karen Ravn*

629. "Who are we? We are children of God. Our potential is unlimited. Our inheritance is sacred. May we always honor that heritage —in every thought and deed."
—Russell M. Nelson

630. "Every problem has in it the seeds of its own solution. If you don't have any problems, you don't get any seeds."
—*Norman Vincent Peale*

631. "Empty pockets never held anyone back. Only empty heads and empty hearts can do that."
—*Norman Vincent Peale*

632. "We are not human beings on a spiritual journey. We are spiritual beings on a human journey."
—Dr. Stephen Covey

633. "Our aspirations are our possibilities."
—Robert Browning

634. "The potential of the average person is like a huge ocean unsailed, a new continent unexplored, a world of possibilities waiting to be released and channeled toward some great good."
—Brian Tracy

635. "Humanity has only scratched the surface of its real potential."
—*Peace Pilgrim*

636. "The most common commodity in this country is unrealized potential."
—*Calvin Coolidge*

637. "It is a denial of the divinity within us to deny our potential and possibilities."
—James E. Faust

638. "No matter what the level of your ability, you have more potential than you can ever develop in a lifetime."
—James T Mccay

639. "Living consciously involves being genuine; it involves listening and responding to others honestly and openly; it involves being in the moment."
—Sidney Poitier

640. "The only limits to the possibilities in your life tomorrow are the buts you use today."
—Les Brown

641. "You are your own scriptwriter and the play is never finished, no matter what your age or position in life."
—Denis Waitley

642. "Life is a great big canvas, and you should throw all the paint on it you can."
—Danny Kaye

643. "Live out of your imagination instead of out of your memory."
—*Les Brown*

644. "If you have zest and enthusiasm you attract zest and enthusiasm. Life does give back in kind."
—*Norman Vincent Peale*

645. "The true sign of intelligence is not knowledge but imagination."
—*Albert Einstein*

646. "Imagination is more important than knowledge. For knowledge is limited to all we now know and understand, while imagination embraces the entire world, and all there ever will be to know and understand."
—*Albert Einstein*

647. "Logic will get you from A to B. Imagination will take you everywhere."
—*Albert Einstein*

648. "Reason can answer questions, but imagination has to ask them."
—*Dr. Ralph Gerard*

649. "This world is but a canvas to our imaginations."
—*Henry David Thoreau*

650. "Things are pretty, graceful, rich, elegant, handsome, but until they speak to the imagination, not yet beautiful."
—*Ralph Waldo Emerson*

651. "Nothing limits achievement like small thinking; nothing expands possibilities like unleashed imagination."
—*William Arthur Ward*

652. "The world of reality has its limits; the world of imagination is boundless."
—*Jean-Jacques Rousseau*

653. "The opportunities of a man are limited only by his imagination. But so few have imagination that there are ten thousand fiddlers to one composer."
—*Charles F. Kettering*

654. "The level of our success is limited only by our imagination and no act of kindness, however small, is ever wasted."
—*Aesop*

655. "There is a space between man's imagination and man's attainment that may only be traversed by his longing."
—*Kahlil Gibran*

656. "I like nonsense, it wakes up the brain cells. Fantasy is a necessary ingredient in living, it's a way of looking at life through the wrong end of a telescope. Which is what I do, and that enables you to laugh at life's realities."
—*Theodore Geisel*

657. "Nothing encourages creativity like the chance to fall flat on one's face."
—*James D. Finley*

658. "My alphabet starts with this letter called yuzz. It's the letter I use to spell yuzz-a-ma-tuzz. You'll be sort of surprised what there is to be found once you go beyond 'Z' and start poking around!."
—*Dr. Seuss*

659. "I believe in the imagination. What I cannot see is infinitely more important than what I can see."
—*Duane Michals*

660. "A rock pile ceases to be a rock pile the moment a single man contemplates it, bearing within him the image of a cathedral."
—*Antoine de Saint-Exupéry*

661. "I saw the angel in the marble and carved until I set him free."
—*Michelangelo*

662. "Think left and think right and think low and think high. Oh, the thinks you can think up if only you try!."
—*Dr. Seuss*

663. "A fool-proof method for sculpting an elephant: first, get a huge block of marble; then you chip away everything that doesn't look like an elephant."
—*Unknown*

664. "The Possible's slow fuse is lit by the Imagination."
—*Emily Dickinson*

665. "I paint objects as I think them, not as I see them."
—*Pablo Picasso*

666. "There are no rules of architecture for a castle in the clouds."
—*G.K. Chesterton*

667. "They who dream by day are cognizant of many things which escape those who dream only by night."
—*Edgar Allan Poe*

668. "Let your imagination release your imprisoned possibilities."
—*Robert H. Schuller*

669. "Things are only impossible until they're not."
—*Jean-Luc Picard, Star Trek: The Next Generation*

670. "Sometimes I've believed as many as six impossible things before breakfast."
—*Lewis Carroll*

671. "When I have a terrible need of—shall I say the word—religion. Then I go out and paint the stars."
—*Vincent Van Gogh*

672. "In the realist you have the sorry sight of the five senses deprived of their imagination."
—*Robert Brault*

673. "When you are describing, A shape, or sound, or tint; Don't state the matter plainly, But put it in a hint; And learn to look at all things, With a sort of mental squint."
—*Lewis Carroll*

674. "Trust that little voice in your head that says 'Wouldn't it be interesting if...' And then do it."
—*Duane Michals*

675. "Live out of your imagination, not your history."
—*Stephen Covey*

PASSION

676. "If you're passionate about what it is you do, then you're going to be looking for everything you can to get better at it."
—*Jack Canfield*

677. "The work of art must seize upon you, wrap you up in itself and carry you away. It is the means by which the artist conveys his passion. It is the current which he puts forth, which sweeps you along in his passion."
—*Pierre-Auguste Renoir*

678. "There is no greatness without a passion to be great, whether it's the aspiration of an athlete or an artist, a scientist, a parent or a business person."
—*Anthony Robbins*

679. "A passion for life is one of the most attractive qualities in a human being. If you want a teammate or a life mate who loves to be around you, all you need to do is love to be around."
—*Denis Waitley*

680. "You have to find something that you love enough to be able to take risks, jump over the hurdles and break through the brick walls that are always going to be placed in front of you. If you don't have that kind of feeling for what it is you're doing, you'll stop at the first giant hurdle."
—*George Lucas*

681. "Your profession is not what brings home your paycheck. Your profession is what you were put on earth to do with such passion and such intensity that it becomes spiritual in calling."
—Vincent Van Gogh

682. "They may forget what you said, but they will never forget how you made them feel."
—*Carl W. Buechner*

683. "Nothing great in the world has ever been accomplished without passion."
—*Hebbel*

684. "A great leader's courage to fulfill his vision comes from passion, not position."
—*John Maxwell*

685. "Most people are other people. Their thoughts are someone else's opinions, their lives a mimicry, their passions a quotation."
—*Oscar Wilde*

686. "Those who danced were thought to be quite insane by those who could not hear the music."
—*Angela Monet*

687. "The way you get meaning into your life is to devote yourself to loving others, devote yourself to your community around you, and devote yourself to creating something that gives you purpose and meaning."
—*Mitch Albom*

688. "The more intensely we feel about an idea or a goal, the more assuredly the idea, buried deep in our subconscious, will direct us along the path to its fulfillment."
—*Earl Nightingale*

689. "Passion, it lies in all of us, sleeping... waiting... and though unwanted... unbidden... it will stir... open its jaws and howl. It speaks to us... guides us... passion rules us all, and we obey. What other choice do we have? Passion is the source of our finest moments. The joy of love... the clarity of hatred... and the ecstasy of grief. It hurts sometimes more than we can bear. If we could live without passion maybe we'd know some kind of peace... but we would be hollow... Empty rooms shuttered and dank. Without passion we'd be truly dead."
—*Joss Whedon*

690. "If there is no passion in your life, then have you really lived? Find your passion, whatever it may be. Become it, and let it become you and you will find great things happen FOR you, TO you and BECAUSE of you."
—*T. Alan Armstrong*

691. "A strong passion for any object will ensure success, for the desire of the end will point out the means."
—*William Hazlitt*

692. "There is no end. There is no beginning. There is only the passion of life."
—*Federico Fellini*

693. "Rest in reason; move in passion."
—*Khalil Gibran*

694. "Passion is the genesis of genius."
—*Anthony Robbins*

695. "Our passions are the winds that propel our vessel. Our reason is the pilot that steers her. Without winds the vessel would not move and without a pilot she would be lost."
—*Proverb*

696. "If passion drives you, let reason hold the reins."
—*Benjamin Franklin*

697. "Chase down your passion like it's the last bus of the night."
—*Terri Guillemets*

698. "Without passion man is a mere latent force and possibility, like the flint which awaits the shock of the iron before it can give forth its spark.
—*Amie*

PATIENCE

699. "Genius is nothing but a great aptitude for patience."
—*George-Louis de Buffon*

700. "Adopt the pace of nature: her secret is patience."
—*Ralph Waldo Emerson*

701. "Patience is the companion of wisdom."
—*St. Augustine*

702. "Patience is also a form of action."
—*Auguste Rodin*

703. "Patience and perseverance have a magical effect before which difficulties disappear and obstacles vanish."
—*John Quincy Adams*

704. "One moment of patience may ward off great disaster. One moment of impatience may ruin a whole life."
—*Chinese Proverb*

705. "Experience has taught me this, that we undo ourselves by impatience. Misfortunes have their life and their limits, their sickness and their health."
—*Michel de Montaigne*

706. "Follow your heart, but be quiet for a while first. Ask questions, then feel the answer. Learn to trust your heart."
—*Unknown*

707. "Be patient toward all that is unsolved in your heart and try to love the questions themselves. Do not now seek the answers, which cannot be given you because you would not be able to live them. And the point is to live everything. Live the questions."
—*Rainer Maria Rilke*

708. "All human wisdom is summed up in two words—wait and hope."
—Alexandre Dumas Père

709. "The two most powerful warriors are patience and time."
—*Leo Nikolaevich Tolstoy*

710. "He that can have Patience, can have what he will."
—*Benjamin Franklin*

711. "Patience is passion tamed."
—*Lyman Abbott*

712. "The key to everything is patience. You get the chicken by hatching the egg, not by smashing it."
—*Arnold H. Glasgow*

713. "Have patience with all things, but chiefly have patience with yourself."
—*St. Francis de Sales*

714. "Patience serves as a protection against wrongs as clothes do against cold. For if you put on more clothes as the cold increases, it will have no power to hurt you. So in like manner you must grow in patience when you meet with great wrongs, and they."
—*Leonardo da Vinci*

715. "Patience is not passive; on the contrary, it is active; it is concentrated strength."
—*Edward G. Bulwer-Lytton*

PERCEPTION

716. "Even a mistake may turn out to be the one thing necessary to a worthwhile achievement."
—*Henry Ford*

717. "We can always choose to perceive things differently. You can focus on what's wrong in your life, or you can focus on what's right."
—*Marianne Williamson*

718. "If the doors of perception were cleansed, everything would appear as it is—infinite."
—*William Blake*

719. "Blessed are they who see beautiful things in humble places where other people see nothing."
—*Camille Pissarro*

720. "People only see what they are prepared to see."
—*Ralph Waldo Emerson*

721. "It is one of the commonest of mistakes to consider that the limit of our power of perception is also the limit of all there is to perceive."
—*C. W. Leadbeater*

722. "There is nothing either good or bad, but thinking makes it so."
—*William Shakespeare*

723. "If you look at your life one way, there is always cause for alarm."
—*Elizabeth Bowen*

724. "What the caterpillar calls the end, the rest of the world calls a butterfly."
—*Lao-tzu*

725. "Pain is a relatively objective, physical phenomenon; suffering is our psychological resistance to what happens. Events may create physical pain, but they do not in themselves create suffering. Resistance creates suffering. Stress happens when your mind resists what is... The only problem in your life is your mind's resistance to life as it unfolds."
—*Dan Millman*

726. "Every exit is an entry somewhere."
—*Tom Stoppard*

727. "The basic difference between an ordinary man and a warrior is that a warrior takes everything as a challenge, while an ordinary man takes everything as a blessing or a curse."
—*Carlos Castaneda*

728. "As you inquire into issues and turn judgments around, you come to see that every perceived problem appearing "out there." is really nothing more than a misperception within your own thinking."
—*Byron Katie*

729. "The trick is in what one emphasizes. We either make ourselves miserable, or we make ourselves strong. The amount of work is the same."
—*Carlos Castaneda*

730. "We cannot choose our external circumstances, but we can always choose how we respond to them."
—*Epictetus*

731. "Man's mind, once stretched by a new idea, never regains its original dimensions."
—*Oliver Wendell Holmes*

732. "The whole world is simply my story, projected back to me on the screen of my own perception. All of it."
—*Byron Katie*

733. "Could we change our attitude, we should not only see life differently, but life itself would come to be different. Life would undergo a change of appearance because we ourselves had undergone a change of attitude."
—*Katherine Mansfield*

734. "If you are distressed by anything external, the pain is not due to the thing itself but to your own estimate of it; and this you have the power to revoke at any moment."
—*Marcus Aurelius*

735. "When the only tool you have is a hammer, all problems begin to resemble nails."
—*Abraham Maslow*

736. "Become a possibilitarian. No matter how dark things seem to be or actually are, raise your sights and see possibilities—always see them, for they're always there."
—*Norman Vincent Peale*

737. "A stumbling block to the pessimist is a stepping-stone to the optimist."
—*Eleanor Roosevelt*

738. "It's not what you look at that matters, it's what you see."
—*Henry David Thoreau*

739. "We choose our joys and sorrows long before we experience them."
—*Kahlil Gibran*

740. "A problem can not be solved with the same consciousness that created it."
—*Albert Einstein*

741. "Reality is merely an illusion, albeit a very persistent one."
—*Albert Einstein*

742. "There are only two ways to live your life. One is as though nothing is a miracle. The other is as though everything is a miracle."
—*Albert Einstein*

743. "We don't see things as they are. We see them as we are."
—*Anais Nin*

744. "A man is as unhappy as he has convinced himself he is."
—*Seneca*

745. "The place one's in, though, doesn't make any contribution to peace of mind: it's the spirit that makes everything agreeable to oneself."
—*Seneca*

746. "Pain is inevitable. Suffering is optional."
—*Dalai Lama*

747. "Nothing is a waste of time if you use the experience wisely."
—*Auguste Rodin*

748. "A verse from the Veda says, 'What you see, you become.' In other words, just the experience of perceiving the world makes you what you are. This is a quite literal statement."
—*Deepak Chopra*

749. "Whatever we focus on is bound to expand. Where we see the negative, we call forth more negative. And where we see the positive, we call forth more positive. Having loved and lost, I now love more passionately. Having won and lost, I now win more soberly. Having tasted the bitter, I now savor the sweet."
—*Marianne Williamson*

750. "You must have absolute faith in your own perceptions of truth. Never act in haste or hurry; be deliberated in everything; wait until you know the true way."
—*Wallace D. Wattles*

751. "Hurry is a manifestation of fear; he who fears not has plenty of time. If you at with perfect faith in your own perceptions of truth, you will never be too late or too early; and nothing will go wrong."
—*Wallace D. Wattles*

PERSISTENCE & PERSEVERENCE

752. "Persistence is a unique mental strength; a strength that is essential to combat the fierce power of the repeated rejections and numerous other obstacles that sit in waiting and are all part of winning in a fast-moving, ever-changing world."
—*Bob Proctor*

753. "You've got to develop mental strength. And you develop mental strength with the will. The will is the mental faculty that gives you the ability to hold one idea under the screen of your mind to the exclusion of all outside distractions."
—*Bob Proctor*

754. "By persisting in your path, though you forfeit the little, you gain the great."
—*Ralph Waldo Emerson*

755. "Most people never run far enough on their first wind to find out if they've got a second. Give your dreams all you've got and you'll be amazed at the energy that comes out of you."
—*William James*

756. "By perseverance the snail reached the ark."
—*Charles H. Spurgeon*

757. "Perseverance is a great element of success. If you only knock long enough and loud enough at the gate, you are sure to wake up somebody."
—*Henry Wadsworth Longfellow*

758. "Nothing is impossible; there are ways that lead to everything, and if we had sufficient will we should always have sufficient means. It is often merely for an excuse that we say things are impossible."
—François de la Rochefoucauld

759. "Never, never, never give up!."
—*Winston Churchill*

760. "Nothing in the world can take the place of persistence. Talent will not; nothing in the world is more common than unsuccessful men with talent. Genius will not; unrewarded genius is a proverb. Education will not; the world is full of educated derelicts. Persistence and determination alone are omnipotent."
—*Calvin Coolidge*

761. "Great works are performed not by strength but by perseverance."
—*Samuel Johnson*

762. "If you are going through hell, keep going."
     —*Winston Churchill*

763. "A champion is someone who gets up, even when he can't."
     —*Jack Dempsey*

764. "Never Quit. Don't ever, ever quit. Recognize that stopping now, regrouping to try a new approach isn't quitting. If you quit you'll regret it forever."
     —*Rudy Ruettiger*

765. "It's not whether you get knocked down; it's whether you get up."
     —*Vince Lombardi*

766. "Let me tell you the secret that has led me to my goal. My strength lies solely in my tenacity."
     —*Louis Pasteur*

767. "When you reach the end of your rope, tie a knot in it and hang on."
     —*Thomas Jefferson*

768. "I think and think for months and years. Ninety-nine times, the conclusion is false. The hundredth time I am right."
     —*Albert Einstein*

769. "Success seems to be largely a matter of hanging on after others have let go."
     —*William Feather*

770. "Consider the postage stamp: its usefulness consists in the ability to stick to one thing till it gets there."
     —*Josh Billings*

771. "The greatest oak was once a little nut who held its ground."
     —*Unknown*

772. "Character consists of what you do on the third and fourth tries."
—*James A. Michener*

773. "Most of the important things in the world have been accomplished by people who have kept on trying when there seemed to be no hope at all."
—*Dale Carnegie*

774. "The difference between perseverance and obstinacy is that one comes from a strong will, and the other from a strong won't."
—*Henry Ward Beecher*

775. "The road to success is dotted with many tempting parking places."
—*Unknown*

776. "Between you and every goal that you wish to achieve, there is a series of obstacles, and the bigger the goal, the bigger the obstacles. Your decision to be, have and do something out of the ordinary entails facing difficulties and challenges that are out of the ordinary as well. Sometimes your greatest asset is simply your ability to stay with it longer than anyone else."
—*Brian Tracy*

777. "Fall seven times, stand up eight."
—*Japanese Proverb*

778. "Perseverance is the hard work you do after you get tired of doing the hard work you already did."
—*Newt Gingrich*

779. "If one dream should fall and break into a thousand pieces, never be afraid to pick one of those pieces up and begin again."
—*Flavia Weedn*

780. "He conquers who endures."
—*Persius*

781. "The great majority of men are bundles of beginnings."
—*Ralph Waldo Emerson*

782. "I returned, and saw under the sun, that the race is not to the swift, nor the battle to the strong, neither yet bread to the wise, nor yet riches to men of understanding, nor yet favour to men of skill; but time and chance happeneth to them all."
—*Ecclesiastes 9:11*

783. "Keep on going, and the chances are that you will stumble on something, perhaps when you are least expecting it. I never heard of anyone ever stumbling on something sitting down."
—*Charles F. Kettering*

784. "Our greatest glory is not in never failing, but in rising up every time we fail."
—*Ralph Waldo Emerson*

785. "Problems are not stop signs, they are guidelines."
—*Robert Schuller*

786. "Vitality shows in not only the ability to persist but the ability to start over."
—*F. Scott Fitzgerald*

787. "With ordinary talent and extraordinary perseverance, all things are attainable."
—*Thomas Foxwell Buxton*

788. "Most people never run far enough on their first wind to find out they've got a second."
—*William James*

789. "Difficult things take a long time, impossible things a little longer."
—André A. Jackson

790. "Don't let the fear of the time it will take to accomplish something stand in the way of your doing it. The time will pass anyway; we might just as well put that passing time to the best possible use."
—*Earl Nightingale*

791. "Stubbornly persist, and you will find that the limits of your stubbornness go well beyond the stubbornness of your limits."
—*Robert Brault*

PROSPERITY

792. "The problem is that most people focus on their failures rather than their successes. But the truth is that most people have many more successes than failures."
—*Jack Canfield*

793. "There are only two words that will always lead you to success. Those words are yes and no. Undoubtedly, you've mastered saying yes. So start practicing saying no. Your goals depend on it!."
—*Jack Canfield*

794. "I have learned this at least by my experiment: that if one advances confidently in the direction of his dreams, and endeavors to live the life he has imagined, he will meet with success unexpected in common hours."
—*Henry David Thoreau*

795. "Formulate and stamp indelibly on your mind a mental picture of yourself as succeeding. Hold this picture tenaciously. Never permit it to fade. Your mind will seek to develop the picture... Do not build up obstacles in your imagination."
—*Norman Vincent Peale*

796. "There is no scarcity of opportunity to make a living at what you love; there's only a scarcity of resolve to make it happen."
—*Wayne Dyer*

797. "Successful people form the habit of doing what failures don't like to do. They like the results they get by doing what they don't necessarily enjoy."
—*Earl Nightingale*

798. "This is the law of prosperity. When apparent adversity comes, be not cast down by it, but make the best of it., and always look forward for better things, for conditions more prosperous."
—*Ralph Waldo Trine*

799. "Any person who contributes to prosperity must prosper in turn."
—*Earl Nightingale*

800. "The more tranquil a man becomes, the greater is his success, his influence, his power for good. Calmness of mind is one of the beautiful jewels of wisdom."
—*James Allen*

801. "The greatest danger for most of us is not that our aim is too high and we miss it, but that it is too low and we reach it."
—*Michelangelo*

802. "If you wait for opportunities to occur, you will be one of the crowd."
—*Edward de Bono*

803. "True prosperity is the result of well-placed confidence in ourselves and our fellow man."
—*Benjamin Burt*

804. "All prosperity begins in the mind and is dependent only on the full use of our creative imagination."
—*Ruth Ross*

805. "Prosperity depends more on wanting what you have than having what you want."
—*Albert F. Geoffrey*

806. "Don't wait for extraordinary opportunities. Seize common occasions and make them great. Weak men wait for opportunities; strong men make them."
—*Orison Swett Marden*

RELATIONSHIPS

807. "Little kindness' and courtesies are so important. In relationships, the little things are the big things."
—*Stephen R. Covey*

808. "The glory of friendship is not the outstretched hand, nor the kindly smile, nor the joy of companionship; it's the spiritual inspiration that comes to one when he discovers that someone else believes in him and is willing to trust him with his friend."
—*Ralph Waldo Emerson*

809. "True friendship comes when the silence between two people is comfortable."
—*David Tyson Gentry*

810. "I just do not hang around anybody that I don't want to be with. Period. For me, that's a blessing, and I can stay positive. I hang around people who are happy, who are growing, who want to learn, who don't mind saying sorry or thank you... and [are] having a fun time."
—*John Assaraf*

811. "A loving relationship is one in which the loved one is free to be himself—to laugh with me, but never at me; to cry with me, but never because of me; to love life, to love himself, to love being loved. Such a relationship is based upon freedom and can never grow in a jealous heart."
—*Leo F. Buscaglia*

812. "Shared joy is a double joy; shared sorrow is half a sorrow."
—*Swedish Proverb*

813. "Remember, we all stumble, every one of us. That's why it's a comfort to go hand in hand."
—*Emily Kimbrough*

814. "There's one sad truth in life I've found While journeying east and west—The only folks we really wound are those we love the best. We flatter those we scarcely know, We please the fleeting guest, And deal full many a thoughtless blow to those who love us best."
—*Ella Wheeler Wilcox*

815. "If you were going to die soon and had only one phone call you could make, who would you call and what would you say? And why are you waiting?"
—*Stephen Levine*

816. "Don't smother each other. No one can grow in the shade."
—*Leo Buscaglia*

817. "Sometimes it is the person closest to us who must travel the furthest distance to be our friend."
—*Robert Brault*

818. "Sticks and stones are hard on bones aimed with angry art, words can sting like anything but silence breaks the heart."
—*Phyllis McGinley*

819. "You can kiss your family and friends good-bye and put miles between you, but at the same time you carry them with you in your heart, your mind, your stomach, because you do not just live in a world but a world lives in you."
—*Frederick Buechner*

820. "Piglet sidled up to Pooh from behind. 'Pooh!' he whispered. 'Yes, Piglet?' 'Nothing,' said Piglet, taking Pooh's paw. 'I just wanted to be sure of you.'"
—*A.A. Milne*

821. "If fame were based on kindness instead of popularity, on understanding and not on worldwide attention, you would be the biggest celebrity on earth. And to my heart, you already are."
—*Anonymous*

822. "Lots of people want to ride with you in the limo, but what you want is someone who will take the bus with you when the limo breaks down."
—*Oprah Winfrey*

823. "You cannot be lonely if you like the person you're alone with."
—*Wayne W. Dyer*

RESPONSIBILITY

824. "Accept responsibility for your life. Know that it is you who will get you where you want to go, no one else."
—*Les Brown*

825. "Promises are like crying babies in a theater, they should be carried out at once."
—*Norman Vincent Peale*

826. "Everything you see happening is the consequence of that which you are."
—Dr. David Hawkins

827. "Let everyone sweep in front of his own door, and the whole world will be clean."
—*Johann Wolfgang von Goethe*

828. "Simply put, you believe that things or people make you unhappy, but this is not accurate. You make yourself unhappy."
—*Wayne Dyer*

829. "Nobody ever did, or ever will, escape the consequences of his choices."
—*Alfred A. Montapert*

830. "You must take personal responsibility. You cannot change the circumstances, the seasons, or the wind, but you can change yourself. That is something you have charge of."
—*Jim Rohn*

831. "Freedom is the will to be responsible to ourselves."
—*Friedrich Nietzsche*

832. "Responsibility is the price of greatness."
—*Winston Churchill*

833. "Life is a gift, and it offers us the privilege, opportunity, and responsibility to give something back by becoming more."
—*Anthony Robbins*

834. "If you want children to keep their feet on the ground, put some responsibility on their shoulders."
—*Abigail Van Buren*

835. "The willingness to accept responsibility for one's own life is the source from which self-respect springs."
—*Joan Didion*

836. "I try to live what I consider a 'poetic existence.' That means I take responsibility for the air I breathe and the space I take up. I try to be immediate, to be totally present for all my work."
—*Maya Angelou*

837. "Nothing strengthens the judgment and quickens the conscience like individual responsibility."
—*Elizabeth Cady Stanton*

838. "Most of us can read the writing on the wall; we just assume it's addressed to someone else."
—*Ivern Ball*

839. "We are alone, with no excuses. That is the idea I shall try to convey when I say that man is condemned to be free. Condemned, because he did not create himself, yet, in other respects is free; because, once thrown into the world, he is responsible for everything he does."
—*Jean-Paul Sartre*

840. "As human beings, we are endowed with freedom of choice, and we cannot shuffle off our responsibility upon the shoulders of God or nature. We must shoulder it ourselves. It is our responsibility."
—*Arnold Toynbee*

841. "Our duty is to preserve what the past has had to say for itself, and to say for ourselves what shall be true for the future."
—*John Ruskin*

842. "If you mess up, 'fess up."
—*Unknown*

843. "When you blame others, you give up your power to change."
—*Unknown*

844. "Even when we know what is right, too often we fail to act. More often we grab greedily for the day, letting tomorrow bring what it will, putting off the unpleasant and unpopular."
—*Bernard M. Baruch*

845. "The best years of your life are the ones in which you decide your problems are your own. You do not blame them on your mother, the ecology, or the president. You realize that you control your own destiny."
—*Albert Ellis*

846. "A new position of responsibility will usually show a man to be a far stronger creature than was supposed."
—*William James*

847. "You are not responsible for the programming you picked up in childhood. However, as an adult, you are one hundred percent responsible for fixing it."
—*Ken Keyes, Jr.*

848. "Few things help an individual more than to place responsibility upon him, and to let him know that you trust him."
—*Booker T. Washington*

849. "Action springs not from thought, but from a readiness for responsibility."
—*Dietrich Bonhoeffer*

850. "No man is fit to comamnd another who cannot command himself."
—*William Penn*

THE LAW OF ATTRACTION

851. "As above, so below. As within, so without."
—*The Emerald Tablet*

852. "Man becomes what he thinks about."
—*Morris Goodman*

853. "You can have, do or be anything you want."
—*Joe Vitale*

854. "You know, when everybody starts to live from their heart, and go for what they want, they don't go for the same things. That's the beauty of this. We don't all want BMWs. We don't all want the same person. We don't all want the same experiences. We don't all want the same clothing. We don't all want... fill in the blank."
—*Joe Vitale*

855. "Take the first step in faith. You don't have to see the whole staircase. Just take the first step."
—*Dr Martin Luther King Jr.*

856. "I believe that you're great, that there's something magnificent about you. Regardless of what has happened to you in your life, regardless of how young or how old you think you might be, the moment you begin to think properly, this something that is within you, this power within you that's greater than the world, it will begin to emerge. It will take over your life. It will feed you, it will clothe you, it will guide you, protect you, direct you, sustain your very existence. If you let it! Now that is what I know, for sure."
—*Michael Beckwith*

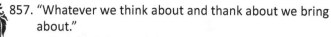

857. "Whatever we think about and thank about we bring about."
—*Dr John F Demartini*

858. "When you visualize, then you materialize. If you've been there in the mind you'll go there in the body."
—*Denis Waitley*

859. "There's enough for everyone. If you believe it, if you can see it, if you act from it, it will show up for you. That's the truth."
—*Michael Beckwith*

860. "Whether you think you can or think you can't, either way you are right."
—*Henry Ford*

861. "Follow your bliss and the universe will open doors for you where there were only walls."
—*Joseph Campbell*

862. "Imagination is everything. It is the preview of life's coming attractions."
—*Albert Einstein*

863. "You want to become aware of your thoughts, you want to choose your thoughts carefully and you want to have fun with this, because you are the masterpiece of your own life. You are the Michelangelo of your own life. The David that you are sculpting is you. And you do it with your thoughts."
—*Joe Vitale*

864. "You can start with nothing. And out of nothing, and out of no way, a way will be made."
—*Michael Beckwith*

865. "We are unlimited beings. We have no ceiling. The capabilities and the talents and the gifts and the power that is within every single individual that is on this planet, is unlimited."
—*Michael Beckwith*

866. "Our feelings are a feedback mechanism to us about whether we're on track or not, whether we're on course or off course. See it's the feeling that really creates the attraction not just the picture or the thought."
—*Jack Canfield*

867. "We are here to change. We are here to grow, develop and unfold. We are progressive beings that have infinite capacity."
—*Michael Beckwith*

868. "Learn to become still. And to take your attention away from what you don't want, and all the emotional charge around it, and place your attention on what you wish to experience."
—*Michael Beckwith*

869. "All that we are is the result of what we have thought. If a man speaks or acts with an evil thought, pain follows him. If a man speaks or acts with a pure thought, happiness follows him, like a shadow that never leaves him."
—*Buddha*

870. "You can begin to shape your own destiny by the attitude that you keep."
—*Michael Beckwith*

871. "You give birth to that on which you fix your mind."
—*Antoine de Saint Exupery*

872. "The greatest discovery of my generation is that human beings can alter their lives by altering their attitudes of mind."
—*William James*

873. "I have found in life that if you want a miracle you first need to do whatever it is you can do—if thats's to plant, then plant; if it is to read, then read; if it is to change, then change; if it is to study, then study; if it is to work, then work; whatever you have to do. And then you will be well on your way of doing the labor that works miracles."
—Jim Rohn

874. "Action will sometimes be required, but if you're really doing it in line with what the universe is trying to deliver, it's going to feel joyous, you're going to feel so alive, time will just stop, you could do it all day."
—Bob Doyle

875. "See yourself living in abundance and you will attract it. It always works, it works every time with every person."
—Bob Proctor

876. "As soon as you start to feel differently about what you already have, you will start to attract more of the good things, more of the things you can be grateful for."
—Joe Vitale

877. "Gratitude is absolutely the way to bring more into your life."
—Marci Shimoff

878. "The best way to predict the future is to create it."
—Peter F. Drucker

879. "You create your own universe as you go along."
—Winston Churchill

880. "It's really important that you feel good. Because this feeling good is what goes out as a signal into the universe and starts to attract more of itself to you. So the more you can feel good, the more you will attract the things that help you feel good and that will keep bringing you up higher and higher."
—Joe Vitale

881. "And you can break yourself free from your hereditary patterns, cultural codes, social beliefs; and prove once and for all that the power within you is greater than the power that's in the world."
—*Michael Beckwith*

882. "The soul attracts that which it secretly harbors; that which it loves, and also that which it fears."
—*James Allen*

883. "Your circumstances may be uncongenial, but they shall not remain so if you only perceive an ideal and strive to reach it. You cannot travel within and stand still without."
—*James Allen*

884. "You are never given a wish without also being given the power to make it true. You may have to work at it, however."
—*Richard Bach*

885. "Our subconscious minds have no sense of humor, play no jokes and cannot tell the difference between reality and an imagined thought or image. What we continually think about eventually will manifest in our lives."
—*Robert Collier*

886. "Whatever you create in your life you must first create in your imagination."
—*Tycho Photiou*

887. "What you resist persists."
—*Carl Jung*

888. "If you're thinking of debt, that's what you're going to attract."
—*Bob Proctor*

889. "He is greatest whose strength carries up the most hearts by the attraction of his own."
—*Henry Ward Beecher*

890. "Whatever you can do, or dream you can, begin it. Boldness has genius, power and magic in it. Begin it now."
—*Johann Wolfgang Von Goethe*

891. "I am no longer cursed by poverty because I took possession of my own mind, and that mind has yielded me every material thing I want, and much more than I need. But this power of mind is a universal one, available to the humblest person as it is to the greatest."
—*Andrew Carnegie*

892. "What lies behind us and what lies before us are tiny matters compared to what lies within us."
—*Ralph Waldo Emerson*

893. "You control your future, your destiny. What you think about comes about. By recording your dreams and goals on paper, you set in motion the process of becoming the person you most want to be. Put your future in good hands—your own."
—*Mark Vistor Hansen*

894. "Every intention sets energy into motion, whether you are conscious of it or not."
—*Gary Zukav*

895. "What power this is I cannot say. All that I know is that it exists."
—*Alexander Graham Bell*

896. "Your mind is a powerful magnet that will attract to you the things you identify yourself with. If you have sad thoughts, you will attract tragedies. If you are a good man, you will attract the company of good people."
—*Alfredo Karras*

THOUGHTS

897. "Let a person radically alter his thoughts, and he will be astonished at the rapid transformation it will effect in the material conditions of his life."
—*James Allen*

898. "It is the nature of thought to find its way into actions."
—*Christian Nevell Bovee*

899. "Creation is always happening. Every time an individual has a thought, or a prolonged, chronic way of thinking, they're in the creation process. Something is going to manifest out of those thoughts."
—*Michael Beckwith*

900. "Change your thoughts and you change your world."
—*Norman Vincent Peale*

901. "The significant problems we face cannot be solved at the same level of thinking we were at when we created them."
—*Albert Einstein*

902. "People become really quite remarkable when they start thinking that they can do things. When they believe in themselves they have the first secret of success."
—*Norman Vincent Peale*

903. "You are a living magnet and you attract into your life the people and the circumstances that are in harmony with your dominant thoughts."
—*Brian Tracy*

904. "Thoughts are sending out that magnetic signal that is drawing the parallel back to you."
—*Joe Vitale*

905. "Your thoughts and your feelings create your life. It will always be that way. Guaranteed."
—*Lisa Nichols*

906. "No problem can withstand the assault of sustained thinking."
—*Voltaire*

907. "Whatever we think about and thank about we bring about."
—*John Demartini*

908. "As a man thinketh, so is he, and as a man chooseth, so is he."
—*Ralph Waldo Emerson*

909. "I attract to my life whatever I give my Attention, Energy and Focus to. Whether wanted or unwanted."
—*Michael Losier*

910. "A clear vision, backed by definite plans, gives you a tremendous feeling of confidence and personal power."
—*Brian Tracy*

911. "What we think determines what happens to us, so if we want to change our lives, we need to stretch our minds."
—*Dr. Wayne Dyer*

912. "Thoughts become things."
—*Mike Dooley*

913. "Our life is what our thoughts make it."
—*Marcus Aurelius*

914. "Change your thoughts, change your life."
—*James Allen*

915. "Our job as humans is to hold on to the thoughts of what we want, make it absolutely clear in our minds what we want, and from that we start to invoke one of the greatest laws in the Universe, and that's the law of attraction. You become what you think about most, but you also attract what you think about most."
—*John Assaraf*

916. "Nurture your mind with great thoughts for you will never go higher than you think."
—*Benjamin Disraeli*

917. "We are what we think. All that we are arises with our thoughts. With our thoughts we make our world."
—*Buddha*

918. "By choosing your thoughts, and by selecting which emotional currents you will release and which you will reinforce, you determine the quality of your Light. You determine the effects that you will have upon others, and the nature of the experiences of your life."
—*Gary Zukav*

919. "Thoughts are the shadows of our feelings—always darker, emptier and simpler."
—*Friedrich Nietzsche*

920. "The ancestor of every action is a thought."
—*Ralph Waldo Emerson*

921. "All intelligent thoughts have already been thought; what is necessary is only to try to think them again."
—*Johann Wolfgang von Goethe*

922. "A man is what he thinks about all day long."
—*Ralph Waldo Emerson*

923. "Thought is the sculptor who can create the person you want to be."
—*Henry David Thoreau*

924. "Always aim at complete harmony of thought and word and deed. Always aim at purifying your thoughts and everything will be well."
—*Mahatma Gandhi*

925. "Thought is the blossom; language the bud; action the fruit behind it."
—*Ralph Waldo Emerson*

926. "You are today where your thoughts have brought you; you will be tomorrow where your thoughts take you."
—*James Allen*

927. "Such as are your habitual thoughts, such also will be the character of your mind; for the soul is dyed by the thoughts."
—*Marcus Aurelius*

928. "Man's greatness lies in his power of thought."
—*Blaise Pascal*

929. "In my garden there is a large place for sentiment. My garden of flowers is also my garden of thoughts and dreams. The thoughts grow as freely as the flowers, and the dreams are as beautiful."
—*Abram L. Urban*

930. "The revelation of thought takes men out of servitude into freedom."
—*Ralph Waldo Emerson*

WEALTH

931. "Wealth is the ability to fully experience life."
—*Henry David Thoreau*

932. "Ordinary riches can be stolen, real riches cannot. In your soul are infinitely precious things that cannot be taken from you."
—*Oscar Wilde*

933. "If you see yourself as prosperous, you will be. If you see yourself as continually hard up, that is exactly what you will be."
—*Robert Collier*

934. "Being rich is having money; being wealthy is having time."
—*Margaret Bonnano*

935. "Only the man who does not need it, is fit to inherit wealth, the man who would make his fortune no matter where he started."
—*Ayn Rand*

936. "If I were to wish for anything, I should not wish for wealth and power, but for the passionate sense of potential—for the eye which, ever young and ardent, sees the possible. Pleasure disappoints; possibility never."
—*Soren Kierkegaard*

937. "Early to bed, early to rise, makes a man healthy, wealthy and wise."
—*Benjamin Franklin*

938. "Wealth is not a matter of intelligence it's a matter of inspiration."
—*Jim Rohn*

939. "I have concluded that wealth is a state of mind, and that anyone can acquire a wealthy state of mind by thinking rich thoughts."
—*Andrew Young*

940. "Wealth, like happiness, is never attained when sought after directly. It comes as a by-product of providing a useful service."
—*Henry Ford*

941. "The greatest wealth is to live content with little."
—*Plato*

942. "The question for each man to settle is not what he would do if he had means, time, influence, and educational advantages, but what he will do with the things he has."
—*Hamilton Wright Mabie*

943. "It is not the creation of wealth that is wrong, but the love of money for its own sake."
—*Margaret Thatcher*

944. "Don't judge men's wealth or godliness by their Sunday appearance."
—*Benjamin Franklin*

945. "They say it is better to be poor and happy than rich and miserable, but how about a compromise like moderately rich and just moody?"
—*Princess Diana*

946. "No man can tell whether he is rich or poor by turning to his ledger. It is the heart that makes a man rich. He is rich or poor according to what he is, not according to what he has."
—*Henry Ward Beecher*

947. "For the majority of instances where money is desired for the admitted object of blessing others, the real underlying motive is a love of popularity, and a desire to pose as a philanthropist or reformer... If your real desire is to do good, there is no need to wait for money before you do it; you can do it now, this very moment, and just where you are."
—*James Allen*

948. "They who are of the opinion that Money will do everything, may very well be suspected to do everything for Money."
—*George Savile*

949. "I'd like to live as a poor man with lots of money."
—*Pablo Picasso*

950. "The real measure of your wealth is how much you'd be worth if you lost all your money."
—*Unknown*

951. "It's good to have money and the things that money can buy, but it's good, too, to check up once in a while and make sure that you haven't lost the things that money can't buy."
—*George Horace Lorimer*

952. "Money is neither my god nor my devil. It is a form of energy that tends to make us more of who we already are, whether it's greedy or loving."
—*Dan Millman*

953. "Money is like manure. You have to spread it around or it smells."
—*J. Paul Getty*

954. "They deem me mad because I will not sell my days for gold; and I deem them mad because they think my days have a price."
—*Kahlil Gibran*

955. "Money isn't the most important thing in life, but it's reasonably close to oxygen on the 'gotta have it' scale."
—*Zig Ziglar*

956. "The little money I have—that is my wealth, but the things I have for which I would not take money, that is my treasure."
—*Robert Brault*

957. "It is neither wealth nor splendor; but tranquility and occupation which give you happiness."
—*Thomas Jefferson*

958. "Wealth is not his that has it, but his that enjoys it."
—*Benjamin Franklin*

959. "He is richest who is content with the least, for content is the wealth of nature."
—*Socrates*

960. "Learning is the beginning of wealth. Learning is the beginning of health. Learning is the beginning of spirituality. Searching and learning is where the miracle process all begins."
—*Jim Rohn*

961. "Whoever renders service to many puts himself in line for greatness—great wealth, great return, great satisfaction, great reputation, and great joy."
—*Jim Rohn*

962. "Wealth is the product of man's capacity to think."
—*Ayn Rand*

963. "All wealth is the product of labor."
—*John Locke*

964. "If we command our wealth, we shall be rich and free; if our wealth commands us, we are poor indeed."
—*Edmund Burke*

965. "All riches have their origin in mind. Wealth is in ideas—not money."
—*Robert Collier*

966. "Money was never a big motivation for me, except as a way to keep score. The real excitement is playing the game."
—*Donald Trump*

967. "Lack of money is the root of all evil."
—*George Bernard Shaw*

WISDOM

968. "Knowing others is intelligence; knowing yourself is true wisdom. Mastering others is strength; mastering yourself is true power."
—*Unknown*

969. "Wise men speak because they have something to say; Fools because they have to say something."
—*Plato*

970. "The well bred contradict other people. The wise contradict themselves."
—*Oscar Wilde*

971. "Wisdom is not a product of schooling but of the lifelong attempt to acquire it."
—*Albert Einstein*

972. "Never mistake knowledge for wisdom. One helps you make a living; the other helps you make a life."
—*Sandra Carey*

973. "God, grant me the serenity to accept the things I cannot change, the courage to change the things I can, and the wisdom to know the difference."
—*Reinhold Niebuhr*

974. "Sometimes I lie awake at night, and ask, 'Where have I gone wrong?' Then a voice says to me, 'This is going to take more than one night.'"
—*Charles M. Schulz*

975. "A man only becomes wise when he begins to calculate the approximate depth of his ignorance."
—*Gian Carlo Menotti*

976. "A wise old owl sat on an oak; The more he saw the less he spoke; The less he spoke the more he heard; Why aren't we like that wise old bird?"
—*Unknown*

977. "The key to wisdom is knowing all the right questions."
—*John A. Simone, Sr.*

978. "The highest form of wisdom is kindness."
—*The Talmud*

979. "Wisdom is knowing what to do next, skill is knowing how to do it, and virtue is doing it."
—*David Starr Jordan*

980. "Wisdom ceases to be wisdom when it becomes too proud to weep, too grave to laugh, and too selfish to seek other than itself."
—*Kahlil Gibran*

981. "The invariable mark of wisdom is to see the miraculous in the common."
—*Ralph Waldo Emerson*

982. "I do not think much of a man who is not wiser today than he was yesterday."
—*Abraham Lincoln*

983. "The next best thing to being wise oneself is to live in a circle of those who are."
—*C.S. Lewis*

984. "Knowing others is wisdom, knowing yourself is enlightenment."
—*Lao Tzu*

985. "Do not brood over your past mistakes and failures as this will only fill your mind with grief, regret and depression. Do not repeat them in the future."
—*Swami Sivananda*

986. "The road of life twists and turns and no two directions are ever the same. Yet our lessons come from the journey, not the destination."
—*Don Williams, Jr.*

987. "Live as if you were to die tomorrow. Learn as if you were to live forever."
—*Mahatma Gandhi*

988. "By three methods we may learn wisdom: first, by reflection, which is noblest; second, by imitation, which is easiest; and third, by experience, which is the most bitter."
—*Confucius*

989. "A wise man makes his own decisions, an ignorant man follows public opinion."
—*Chinese Proverbs*

990. "A word to the wise ain't necessary, it's the stupid ones who need the advice."
—*Bill Cosby*

991. "A man begins cutting his wisdom teeth the first time he bites off more than he can chew."
—*Herb Caen*

992. "Honesty is the first chapter in the book of wisdom."
—*Thomas Jefferson*

993. "The art of being wise is the art of knowing what to overlook."
—*William James*

994. "The more sand that has escaped from the hourglass of our life, the clearer we should see through it."
—*Jean Paul*

995. "The young man knows the rules, but the old man knows the exceptions."
—*Oliver Wendell Holmes*

996. "To be satisfied with a little, is the greatest wisdom; and he that increaseth his riches, increaseth his cares; but a contented mind is a hidden treasure, and trouble findeth it not."
—*Akhenaton*

997. "We are made wise not by the recollection of our past, but by the responsibility for our future."
—*George Bernard Shaw*

998. "When I can look life in the eyes, grown calm and very coldly wise, life will have given me the truth, and taken in exchange—my youth."
—*Sara Teasdale*

999. "Wisdom is found only in truth."
—*Johann Wolfgang von Goethe*

1000. "Wisdom is not wisdom when it is derived from books alone."
—*Horace*

1001. "Wisdom is the reward you get for a lifetime of listening when you'd have preferred to talk."
—*Doug Larson*

APPENDIX

The Smartest Words Ever Spoken makes an excellent gift for:

- friends
- family
- fund raisers
- sales promotions
- speech preparation

For quantity discounts, please contact :
sales@abcpublishing.org

To join the discussion and get daily quotes, join my Facebook page at:
http://www.facebook.com/ConceiveBelieveAchieve

Order online at http://SmartestWordsEverSpoken.com

NOTES

Made in the USA
Lexington, KY
24 April 2012